SHAY GEARED LOCOMOTIVES AND REPAIR PARTS
CATALOGUE

©2008-2010 Periscope Film LLC
All Rights Reserved
ISBN #978-1-935327-92-9   1-935327-92-5
www.PeriscopeFilm.com

SHAY GEARED LOCOMOTIVES

30 CHURCH ST.   NEW YORK CITY.
WORKS: LIMA, OHIO.

NORTHWESTERN REPRESENTATIVES:
HOFIUS STEEL & EQUIPMENT COMPANY,
L.C. SMITH BUILDING,
SEATTLE, WASHINGTON.

SOUTHERN REPRESENTATIVES:
WOODWARD, WIGHT & COMPANY,
NEW ORLEANS,
LOUISIANA.

SOUTHWESTERN REPRESENTATIVES.
NORMAN B. LIVERMORE & COMPANY,
1306 MERCHANTS' NATIONAL BANK BLDG.,
SAN FRANCISCO, CALIFORNIA.

MEXICAN REPRESENTATIVES:
INTERNATIONAL RAILWAY SUPPLY COMPANY,
30 CHURCH STREET,
NEW YORK CITY.

THE GENERAL SUPPLY COMPANY, S.A.
AV. ISABEL LA CATOLICA NO. 51,
MEXICO CITY.

CABLE ADDRESS: SHAYLOCO NEW YORK.
CODES, WESTERN UNION, LIEBERS, A.B.C. 5TH. EDITION, MCNEIL'S.

LIMA LOCOMOTIVE WORKS, INCORPORATED, LIMA, OHIO

SHAY GEARED LOCOMOTIVES

GENERAL DESIGN

THE designs illustrated and described in this catalogue comprise our standard Shay Geared Locomotives. These fulfill all the requirements of ordinary industrial and logging operations. To meet special conditions, our engineers will be glad to co-operate with customers in the production of designs to meet their special requirements. Our engineering department is ready at all times to furnish information, and to advise as to the most satisfactory designs for particular conditions.

Shay Geared Locomotives operate successfully under extraordinary conditions of track and grade. These engines are built in sizes ranging from 13 tons up to any size to meet customers' requirements. From 20 tons up, the locomotive is constructed with three cylinders. This gives a constant torque and produces an even and powerful exhaust. This last feature makes the engine steam freely.

The boilers are carefully designed, and provided with large steam spaces, so that they will operate satisfactorily on steep grades.

The frames are made of Standard I-beam sections, or of the girder type. The trucks are solidly built, and thoroughly braced. *All wheels are driving wheels, and the total weight of both engine and tender is used to pull the load. Therefore, a Shay Locomotive of the same weight as a direct locomotive and its tender will produce a much greater draw-bar pull.*

Due to the fact that there is no counterbalance in the driving wheels, there is a total absence of dynamic augment, or what is commonly known as "hammerblow" on the rail. *Because of this, the Shay Geared Locomotive operates on track too light for a direct engine of the same axle load.* It is easy on the track and reduces very materially the cost of repairs and upkeep.

As shown by the accompanying illustrations, the wheels are driven by means of gears connected on the driving crank shaft, which is applied to the right side of the engine. To compensate for curves the driving shafts are of an ingenious design provided with universal couplings and slip joints. *The whole construction accommodates itself very freely to curves and uneven track.*

FIFTY TON SHAY AT OKLAHOMA PORTLAND CEMENT COMPANY

Another particularly desirable feature of the Shay, when operating on bad track, is the ease with which it can be replaced upon the rails. For ordinary derailment, when only one truck is off, the engine can be easily and quickly put back upon the track by its own power and the use of common wrecking frogs. It is unusual to require the assistance of another engine to help a Shay on to the track after derailment.

It has been demonstrated that a Shay Locomotive is so simple in construction and easy to operate that any man who has had experience in stationary plant work can learn very quickly to become a competent Shay engineer.

SERVICE FOR WHICH THE SHAY IS ADAPTED

The Shay Geared Locomotive has a wide and varied range of service, being used in industrial, quarry, contractor's, logging, mining and plantation work, also on branch lines and mountain sections of trunk-line railways.

It is especially adapted to industrial railroads in and around large manufacturing plants. Its value as a switching engine is due to the rapidity with which it will accelerate a load and to its ability to spot cars at given points in a minimum of time. It is designed to take any curve on which standard cars can be operated.

For use on heavy grades, sharp curves and light rails, it is particularly desirable. The large number of exhausts at slow speeds produces a steady draft. This gives the Shay Locomotive excellent steaming qualities and tends to reduce the consumption of fuel to a minimum.

SIXTY TON SHAY AT MORGAN & WRIGHT PLANT, DETROIT, MICH.

The Shay Locomotive has the greatest hauling capacity, in comparison with its weight, of any locomotive.

It is the most economical and efficient heavy duty locomotive so far produced for the classes of service above designated.

DETERMINING SIZE OF LOCOMOTIVE REQUIRED

In order to determine the size of locomotive which will be the most advantageous for the customer to purchase, we should be given all facts relative to the conditions under which the locomotive will be required to operate.

This information should cover length of road, gauge, fuel used, weight of rail, per cent. of steepest grade, radius of sharpest curve, kind of cars used, weight of cars empty and loaded, number of cars to be handled per trip, and whether loaded or empty cars are to be hauled over grade.

To aid customers in giving this information we have prepared an information blank, which will be found in the back of this catalogue. With this information we can prepare specifications and submit a proposition on a locomotive of the proper size to perform the work required.

Where the road has not been completed, or operations started, which would make it impossible to give complete information, the customer should estimate the conditions as closely as possible and answer questions accordingly.

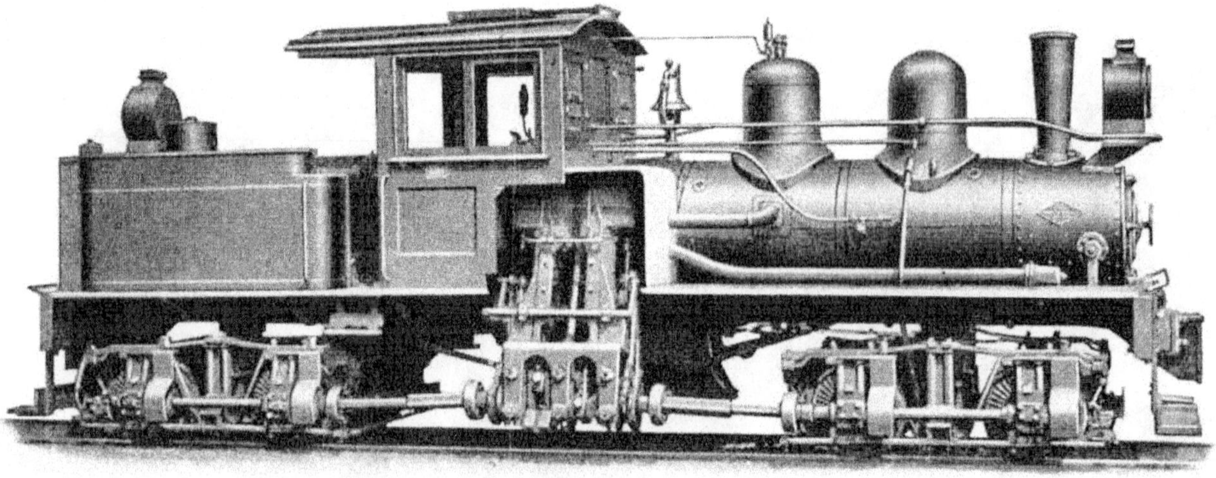

CLASS "A" SHAY LOCOMOTIVES

Code Word	Weight in Working Order	Boiler Pressure	Cylinders			Wheel Base			Drivers		Capacity of Water Tank	Fuel Capacity, Coal	Fuel Capacity, Wood	Fuel Capacity, Oil	Tractive Power	Hauling Capacity in Tons of 2,000 Lbs. (Exclusive of Engine)							
			No.	Diam.	Stroke	Rigid	Total		No.	Diam.						On Level	On Grades—Straight Track						
																	½%	1%	2%	3%	4%	5%	6%
	Tons	Lbs.		In.	In.	In.	Ft.	In.		In.	Gals.	Tons	Cords	Gals.	Lbs.								
ABE	13	160	2	6	10	48	18	10	8	22	400	¾	½	125	6050	643	326	203	113	76	55	43	34
ABLE	18	160	2	7	12	50	21	0	8	29	730	1	¾	285	7480	914	395	246	135	88	64	48	37

NOTE.—All hauling capacities given above are based on 8 lbs. per ton rolling friction, and mean effective pressure 75% of full boiler pressure.

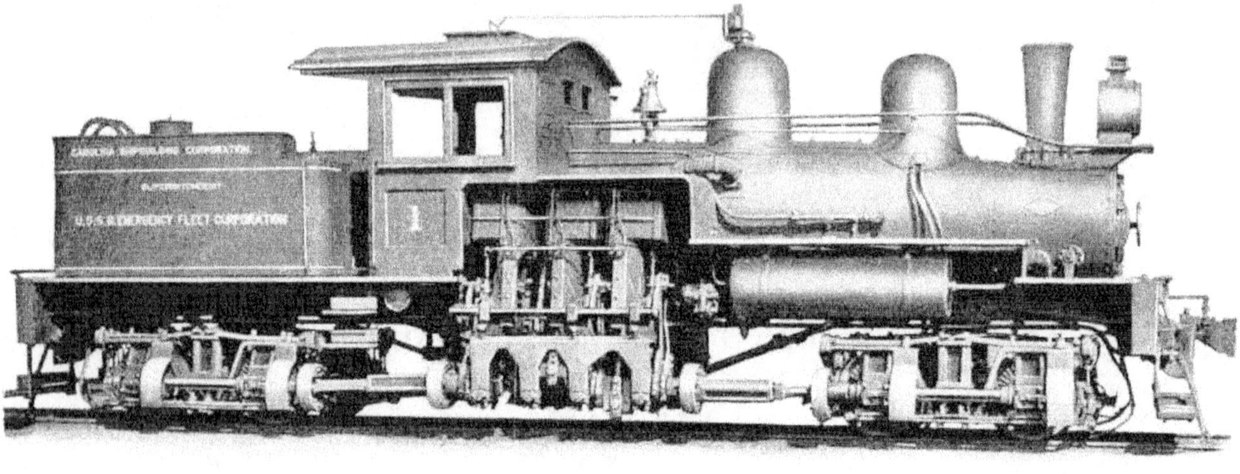

CLASS "B" SHAY LOCOMOTIVES

Code Word	Weight in Working Order	Boiler Pressure	Cylinders			Wheel Base			Drivers		Capacity of Water Tank	Fuel Capacity, Coal	Fuel Capacity, Wood	Fuel Capacity, Oil	Tractive Power	Hauling Capacity in Tons of 2,000 Lbs. (Exclusive of Engine)							
			No.	Diam.	Stroke	Rigid	Total		No.	Diam.						On Level	On Grades—Straight Track						
																	½%	1%	2%	3%	4%	5%	6%
	Tons	Lbs.		In.	In.	In.	Ft.	In.		In.	Gals.	Tons	Cords	Gals.	Lbs.								
BA	20	160	3	6	12	50	23	6	8	29	730	1	¾	285	8600	1055	457	287	158	106	78	59	47
BAY	24	160	3	8	8	50	24	1	8	29	830	1¼	1	500	9750	1193	518	325	179	119	87	66	52
BALE	28	160	3	8	10	50	24	4	8	29	850	1½	1¼	500	12200	1498	650	407	226	152	111	85	67
BALER	32	160	3	8	12	50	25	5	8	29	1000	1¾	1½	500	13500	1655	718	451	249	167	121	93	73
BALLAD	36	180	3	10	10	50	26	5	8	29	1200	1¾	1½	800	14320	1756	760	476	262	174	126	96	76
BALLOON	42	180	3	10	12	50	27	2	8	29½	1560	2	1¾	800	16900	2070	898	562	310	206	150	114	90
BALUSTER	50	200	3	11	12	52	28	10	8	32	1750	3¼	2	950	22580	2775	1205	767	421	282	206	159	126
BALUSTRAD	60	200	3	12	12	56	33	4	8	36	2000	3¼	2	1200	23890	2928	1267	793	438	291	211	161	127
BALUSTRUT	70	200	3	13	15	60	34	10	8	40	3000	5	2½	1500	32480	3985	1730	1083	602	402	294	225	179

NOTE.—All hauling capacities given above are based on 8 lbs. per ton rolling friction, and mean effective pressure 75% of full boiler pressure.

LIMA SHAY GEARED LOCOMOTIVES

CLASS "C" SHAY LOCOMOTIVES

Code Word	Weight in Working Order	Boiler Pressure	Cylinders			Wheel Base		Drivers		Capacity of Water Tank	Fuel Capacity, Coal	Fuel Capacity, Wood	Fuel Capacity, Oil	Tractive Power	Hauling Capacity in Tons of 2,000 Lbs. (Exclusive of Engine)							
			No.	Diam.	Stroke	Rigid	Total	No.	Diam.						On Level	On Grades—Straight Track						
																1%	1½%	2%	3%	4%	5%	6%
	Tons	Lbs.		In.	In.	In.	Ft. In.		In.	Gals.	Tons	Cords	Gals.	Lbs.								
Ca	60	200	3	11	12	52	35 6	12	32	2000	3½	2	1200	25830	3165	1372	862	479	320	234	179	142
Cap	70	200	3	12	15	52	40 2	12	36	3000	5	2½	1200	30350	3723	1616	1014	562	376	275	211	167
Care	80	200	3	13½	15	56	44 6	12	36	3000	5	2½	1200	35100	4305	1868	1169	648	434	317	242	192
Carat	90	200	3	14½	15	56	43 3½	12	36	3500	5	2½	1500	40400	4960	2156	1353	752	504	369	284	225
Carbon	100	200	3	15	17	58	45 6	12	40	4000	6		1500	44100	5411	2349	1470	819	548	400	308	244
Capture	125	200	3	17	18	64	46 10	12	46	4000	9		2000	53000	6500	2817	1768	979	654	477	366	289

NOTE.—All hauling capacities given above are based on 8 lbs. per ton rolling friction, and mean effective pressure 75% of full boiler pressure.

CLASS "D" SHAY LOCOMOTIVES

Code Word	Weight in Working Order	Boiler Pressure	Cylinders			Wheel Base		Drivers		Capacity of Water Tank	Fuel Capacity, Coal	Fuel Capacity, Oil	Tractive Power	Hauling Capacity in Tons of 2,000 Lbs. (Exclusive of Engine)							
			No.	Diam.	Stroke	Rigid	Total	No.	Diam.					On Level	On Grades—Straight Track						
															1%	1½%	2%	3%	4%	5%	6%
	Tons	Lbs.		In.	In.	In.	Ft. In.		In.	Gals.	Tons	Gals.	Lbs.								
Dan	150	200	3	17	18	64	58 4	16	46	8000	9	2000	53000	5475	2792	1743	954	629	452	341	264

NOTE.—All hauling capacities given above are based on 8 lbs. per ton rolling friction, and mean effective pressure 75% of full boiler pressure.

STANDARD SPECIFICATIONS FOR ALL LOCOMOTIVES

With each proposition for locomotives we furnish a detailed specification giving all the important dimensions. Particular attention is paid to locomotives required to work under unusual or severe conditions, and the designs are made to meet the case. We are prepared to build Shay Locomotives to burn hard and soft coal, coke, wood of all varieties, and oil. The fire-box, grates, dampers, front-end arrangement, and stack are changed to suit the fuel desired.

Each wood or coal burning locomotive is supplied with the following tools:

1 Water-Gauge Glass Lamp	1 Wood or Clinker Hook	1 Sample Can of Grease
1 Cab Lamp	1 Coal Pick	1 Water Glass
1 Torch	1 Coal Shovel	Wrenches for all Nuts
1 Cape Chisel	2 Locomotive Jackscrews	1 Valve Tram
1 Cold Chisel	1 Pair Wrecking Frog and Wedge	2 Seat Boxes
1 Hard (Machinist's) Hammer	1 Tallow Pot	2 Cushions
1 Soft (Copper) Hammer	1 Spare Set of Piston-Rod Packing	1 Packing Hook
1 Combination Pipe and Monkey Wrench	1 Hand Oil Can	1 Packing Spade
1 Pinch Bar	1 One-gallon Oil Can	1 Square Bar
1 Flue Scraper	5 lbs. of Waste	2 Jack Bars
1 Ash Hoe	1 Sample Can of Oil	1 Spanner Wrench

SPECIAL EQUIPMENT

The following items are not regularly furnished, but can be applied to locomotives for a reasonable extra charge:

Extra Headlight	Lima R. & H. Stack
Air Brake	Diamond Stack
Electric Headlights	Superheater
Acetylene Headlights	Firebrick Arch
Fire Extinguisher	Wide Tires

MATERIAL

All material entering into the construction of Shay Locomotives is made to conform to the latest approved practice of railroads and locomotive builders and is in accordance with the latest requirements of the American Society for Testing Materials and Railway Master Mechanics' Association.

The Lima Locomotive Works, Incorporated, has a testing department with men in charge who are thoroughly familiar with locomotive requirements and capable of making complete chemical analyses and physical tests of all material entering into locomotive construction.

The laboratories are equipped with modern testing machines and approved apparatus for chemical analyses.

On each locomotive this work is followed closely by our Chemist and Engineer of Tests. A suitable record is kept of all tests made so that we know the quality of all material used in our product.

TABLE OF STANDARD AND MINIMUM DIMENSIONS

Radius of Sharpest Curves Advised and Practicable. Weight Rail Advised for Different Weight Shay Locomotives.

Code Word	Weight of Locomotive in Working Order	Standard Dimensions: Height of Locomotive above Rail		Standard Dimensions: Length of Engine and Tender		Standard Dimensions: Gauge	Minimum Dimensions: Minimum Height of Locomotive above Rail		Minimum Dimensions: Minimum Gauge for which Locomotive can be Built	Radius Sharpest Curve Advised	Radius Sharpest Curve Practicable with Standard Construction	Weight of Lightest Rail Advised
	Tons	Ft.	In.	Ft.	In.	In.	Ft.	In.	In.	Ft.	Ft.	Lbs.
Abe	13	9	0	25	4	56½	7	4	24	50	45	12
Able	18	10	8½	29	2	56½	9	1	24	50	50	16
Ba	20	10	11½	31	2	56½	9	4	24	50	50	20
Bay	24	11	3½	33	2	56½	9	6	24	75	65	20
Bale	28	11	6¼	33	2	56½	9	9	30	75	70	25
Baler	32	11	8	34	7	56½	9	11	30	75	70	25
Ballad	36	12	3	35	5	56½	10	9	30	75	75	30
Balloon	42	12	9¾	36	6	56½	11	4	30	75	75	35
Baluster	50	13	2¾	39	6	56½	11	9	36	100	90	45
Balustrad	60	13	11	46	7	56½	12	5	42	100	90	55
Balustrut	70	13	7½	45	10	56½	13	1	56½	100	100	60
Ca	60	13	2¾	47	2	56½	11	9	36	100	100	45
Cap	70	14	4	52	9	56½	12	10	36	100	100	45
Care	80	12	6	58	6	56½	12	7	56½	100	100	60
Carat	90	13	10½	56	3	56½	12	10	56½	100	100	60
Carbon	100	13	10½	58	11	56½	13	0	56½	100	100	65
Capture	125	14	4	61	6	56½	14	4	56½	100	100	70
Dan	150	14	4	72	4	56½	14	4	56½	125	125	70

The limitations given in the table are for Standard Shay Locomotives only. If conditions require limitations less than the above, kindly give us full details, and we will advise if they can be met.

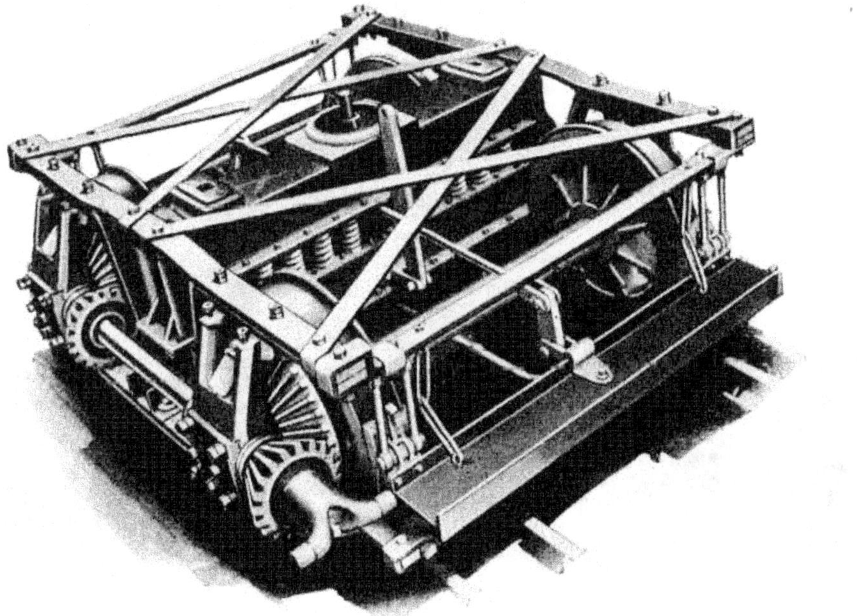

All Steel Built-Up Shay Locomotive Truck

12 LIMA SHAY GEARED LOCOMOTIVES

100 Ton Shay Locomotive Equipped with Locomotive Superheater

Cast Steel Truck — Shay Locomotive

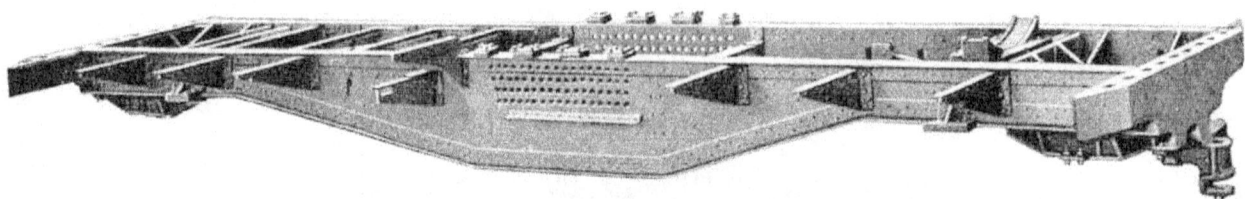

Steel Girder Frame

160 Ton Shay Locomotive — Kansas City Southern Railway

LIMA SHAY GEARED LOCOMOTIVES

Shay Locomotives work on the roughest track or sharpest curve a car can take

SHAY LOCOMOTIVES

SHAY GEARED LOCOMOTIVE FOR INDUSTRIAL RAILWAYS

Tests to determine the relative amount of work accomplished by Shays and rod engines of the same tractive power were made by the Lima Locomotive Works, Inc., April 14, 1917. We made these tests because we had to know. We build both Shay and Rod engines.

These tests were made with an 0-6-0 type engine and a Shay of equal tractive effort.

Two series of runs were made with the engines operated at maximum tractive effort by experienced engineers.

The purpose of test No. 1 was to obtain comparative rates of acceleration of the two engines when working under exactly the same conditions of road and track.

The purpose of test No. 2 was to determine the time required by the two engines to spot a given load at definite points.

CONCLUSIONS

The value of an industrial locomotive depends upon
    1st. Its ability to spot accurately the load at given points in a minimum time.
    2nd. Its ability quickly to accelerate loads.

IN INDUSTRIAL SERVICE

These tests show Shay engines to be 11 per cent. quicker and more accurate at spotting cars and to average 22 per cent. less time in attaining a speed of 12 miles per hour.

	WEIGHT APPROXIMATE	RELATIVE WORK AS SWITCHER
Shay	50 tons loaded	110%
0-6-0 type with tender	90 tons engine and tender	100%
0-6-0 type saddle tank	54 tons loaded	100%

Here is the Test Track with Distances Marked by Posts

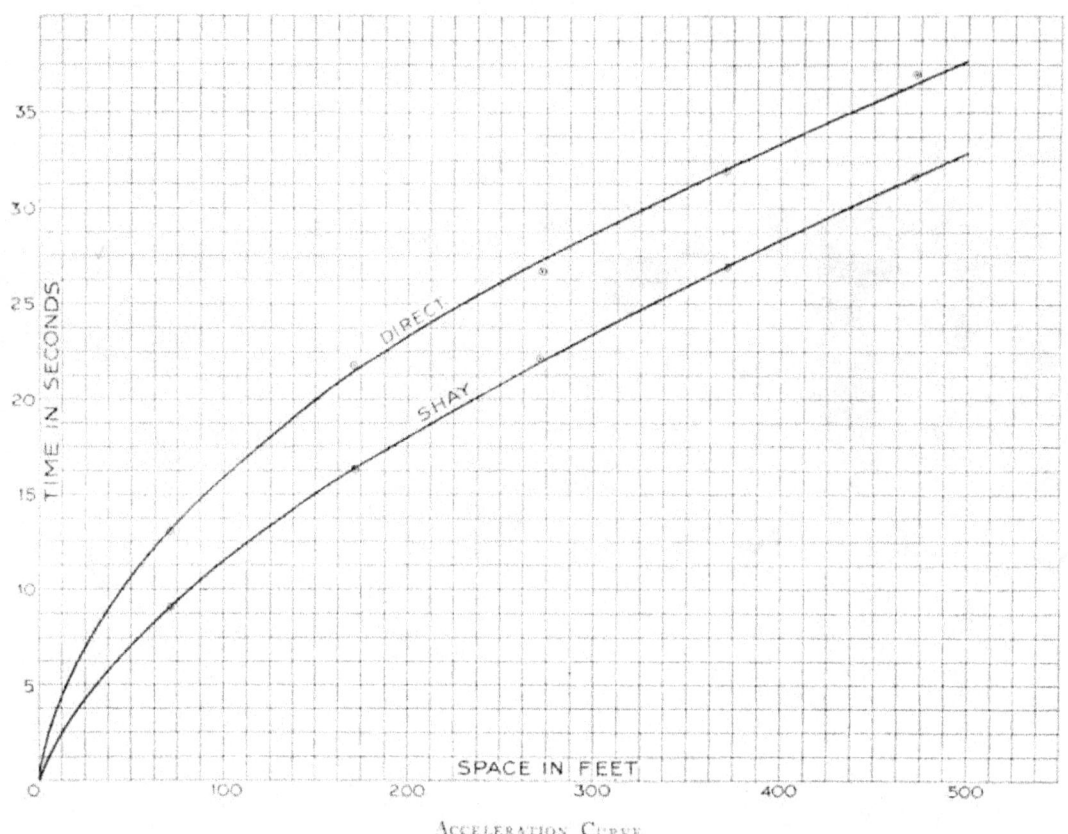

Acceleration Curve

ACCELERATION TEST

These test runs were made over a 500-foot length of track from a standing start up to running speed. The front bumper of the engine was opposite stake No. 1 at the start and the time at which the cab passed each stake was noted. The average time of three consecutive runs were used for the final result.

The results of this test plotted from direct time observations is shown in the acceleration curve. A comparison of the values for distance and time is tabulated below.

From standing start up to	100 ft.	200 ft.	300 ft.	400 ft.	500 ft.
Time required by Shay (seconds)	11½	18	23½	28½	32¾
Time required by direct (seconds)	16	23¼	28¾	33¼	37½
Time saved by Shay	28%	22½%	18¼%	14¼%	12¾%

This test clearly shows the Shay locomotive to have a higher initial acceleration than the rod locomotive. It will get up to the same speed in less time. The actual time saved varies from 13 per cent. to 28 per cent., depending upon the length of the run. In getting up to a speed of 12 miles per hour, an average rate for switching, Shay locomotives require 22 per cent. less time than a rod connected locomotive.

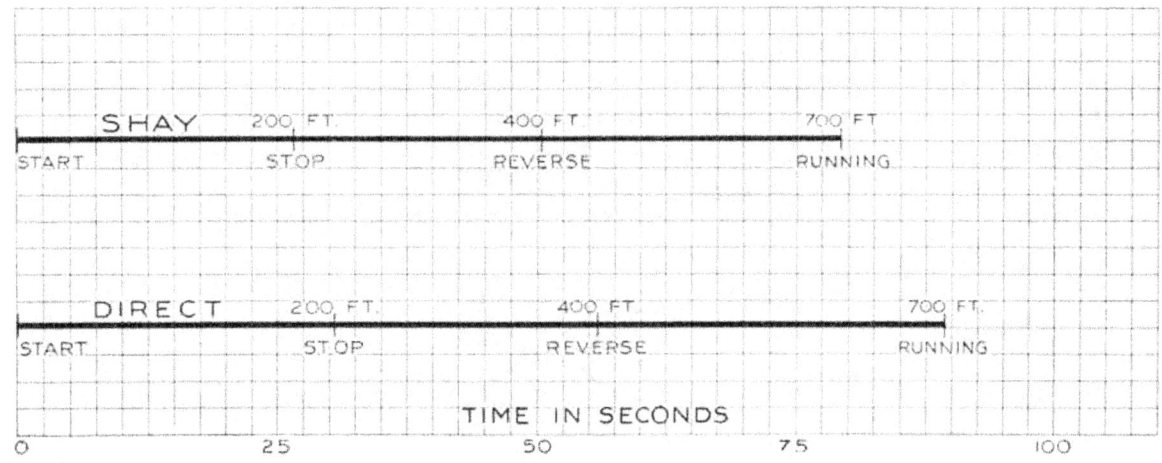

Spotting Chart

SPOTTING TEST

For this test, runs were made over a 700-foot length of track. The engine was run for 200 feet and stopped. Then started and run 200 feet further, reversed and run back 300 feet. The time was noted at the start, when stopped, when reversed, and when passing the 300-feet stake on the return. The average of three consecutive runs is shown in the final result.

This test shows that the Shay locomotive started and stopped in a space of 200 feet in 13 per cent. less time than the rod locomotive. Then starting again, reversing at 200 feet and running back 300 feet, the Shay locomotive took 11 per cent. less time than the rod locomotive. From the first start until it had run 700 feet, including one stop and one reverse, the Shay locomotive required about 11 per cent. less time. In all cases the Shay locomotive spotted locations more accurately than the rod locomotive.

Forty-Two Ton Shay—The Lunkenheimer Co.

METHOD OF DETERMINING THE RADIUS OF A CURVE

When the radius of a curve is not known, the following method can be used to determine it. Select two points on the inside of the head of the inside rail, corresponding to A and B in the diagram

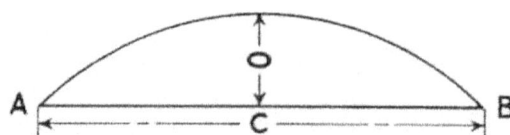

Measure the distance between these points. Stretch a line between the two points A and B and measure the distance from this line to the inside of the rail head at a point midway between these points corresponding to "O" in the diagram. These dimensions to be measured in feet or inches. With the above measurements the radius of curve can be obtained by the following formula:

$$\text{Radius of curve} = \tfrac{1}{2}\left(\frac{\tfrac{1}{2}C^2}{O} + O\right)$$

To insure against any error in the measurements due to irregularities in the tracks, it is always better to take measurements at several parts of the curve.

When the radius of the curve is given in feet and is required to be converted to degrees, an approximate formula is:

$$D = \frac{57.3°}{R}$$

D = curvature, in degrees
R = radius of curve, in feet

RESISTANCE

The total resistance offered to the passage of a train is composed of rolling friction, grade resistance, and curve resistance. Rolling friction depends on the weight per axle, the speed, the method of lubrication, the condition of the track, etc. A good general figure as an average for speeds under 20 miles per hour, is from 8 to 10 pounds per ton, although with heavy cars and the best of track conditions the rolling friction may be found to be less. For poor conditions of track and lubrication it may reach 20 pounds, and for mine cars with loose wheels, etc., it is sometimes 50 pounds per ton. The resistance due to speed is of little or no importance in freight traffic, having practically no effect at speeds under 20 miles per hour. The curve resistance is approximately ½ pound per ton for each degree of curvature. The grade resistance is 20 pounds per ton for each per cent. of grade.

The following is an example to determine the size locomotive required, with given conditions:

Grade	1½ per cent.
Curves	16 degree
Load	300 tons
Grade Resistance	20 × 1½ × 300 = 9,000
Rolling Friction	8 × 300 = 2,400
Curve Resistance	8 × 300 = 2,400
Total Resistance of Train	13,800

Assume a 42-ton Shay Locomotive to do this work. To obtain the tractive power required the total resistance of the locomotive must be added.

Resistance of Locomotive

Grade	20 × 1½ × 42 = 1,260
Rolling Friction	8 × 42 = 336
Curve	8 × 42 = 336
Total Resistance of Locomotive	1,932

The resistance of the train load plus the resistance of locomotive will equal tractive power required:

$$13,800 + 1,932 = 15,732, \text{ Total Tractive Power Required}$$

The tractive power of our standard 42-ton engine is 16,900 pounds. From this it will be seen that the standard 42-ton engine will handle the load on the grade and curve as given above.

TABLE OF DEGREE OF CURVES AND RADIUS

Degree of Curve	Radius in Feet	Length of Chord in Feet 30	Length of Chord in Feet 20	Degree of Curve	Radius in Feet	Length of Chord in Feet 30	Length of Chord in Feet 20
		Ordinate in Inches	Ordinate in Inches			Ordinate in Inches	Ordinate in Inches
10	574	2.36	1.04	47	126	10.90	4.85
11	522	2.50	1.15	48	123	11.08	4.94
12	478	2.83	1.26	49	121	11.30	5.04
13	442	3.05	1.36	50	119	11.52	5.13
14	410	3.30	1.46	52	115	11.92	5.31
15	383	3.54	1.57	54	111	12.36	5.52
16	359	3.76	1.67	56	107	12.84	5.72
17	338	4.00	1.78	58	104	13.22	5.92
18	320	4.21	1.87	60	100	13.68	6.12
19	303	4.45	1.98	62	97.08	14.04	6.24
20	288	4.70	2.09	64	94.35	14.40	6.48
21	274	4.92	2.18	66	91.80	14.88	6.60
22	262	5.16	2.29	68	89.41	15.24	6.72
23	251	5.40	2.39	70	87.17	15.60	6.84
24	241	5.64	2.50	72	85.06	15.96	7.08
25	231	5.83	2.59	74	83.08	16.32	7.20
26	222	6.07	2.70	76	81.20	16.80	7.44
27	214	6.29	2.80	78	79.45	17.16	7.56
28	207	6.54	2.90	80	77.78	17.52	7.80
29	200	6.77	3.00	85	74.00	18.48	8.16
30	194	7.08	3.12	90	70.71	19.32	8.52
31	188	7.32	3.24	95	67.81	20.16	8.88
32	182	7.56	3.36	100	65.27	21.00	9.36
33	176	7.80	3.48	105	63.02	21.72	9.60
34	171	7.96	3.60	110	61.04	22.56	9.96
35	167	8.16	3.69	115	59.28	23.16	10.20
36	162	8.40	3.78	120	57.73	23.76	10.44
37	158	8.64	3.86	125	56.36	24.48	10.80
38	154	8.88	3.96	130	55.17	24.96	10.92
39	150	9.12	4.08	135	54.12	25.56	11.28
40	147	9.36	4.16	140	53.21	25.92	11.40
41	143	9.60	4.27	145	52.43	26.28	11.52
42	140	9.82	4.38	150	51.76	26.64	11.76
43	137	10.04	4.49	160	50.77	27.24	12.00
44	134	10.32	4.58	170	50.19	27.60	12.12
45	131	10.50	4.67	180	50.00	27.62	12.13
46	128	10.68	4.76				

COMPARISON OF DIFFERENT METHODS OF DESIGNATING THE SAME GRADE

Per Cent. of Grade	Grade in Feet per Mile	Per Cent. of Grade	Grade in Feet per Mile
⅛ of 1 per cent. or 1½ inches per 100 feet	= 6.6 feet per mile	4½ per cent. or 4 feet 6 inches per 100 feet	= 237.6 feet per mile
¼ of 1 per cent. or 3 inches per 100 feet	= 13.2 feet per mile	4¾ per cent. or 4 feet 9 inches per 100 feet	= 250.8 feet per mile
½ of 1 per cent. or 6 inches per 100 feet	= 26.4 feet per mile	5 per cent. or 5 feet 0 inches per 100 feet	= 264.0 feet per mile
¾ of 1 per cent. or 9 inches per 100 feet	= 39.6 feet per mile	5¼ per cent. or 5 feet 3 inches per 100 feet	= 277.2 feet per mile
1 per cent. or 1 foot 0 inches per 100 feet	= 52.8 feet per mile	5½ per cent. or 5 feet 6 inches per 100 feet	= 290.4 feet per mile
1¼ per cent. or 1 foot 3 inches per 100 feet	= 66.0 feet per mile	5¾ per cent. or 5 feet 9 inches per 100 feet	= 303.6 feet per mile
1½ per cent. or 1 foot 6 inches per 100 feet	= 79.2 feet per mile	6 per cent. or 6 feet 0 inches per 100 feet	= 316.8 feet per mile
1¾ per cent. or 1 foot 9 inches per 100 feet	= 92.4 feet per mile	6¼ per cent. or 6 feet 3 inches per 100 feet	= 330.0 feet per mile
2 per cent. or 2 feet 0 inches per 100 feet	= 105.6 feet per mile	6½ per cent. or 6 feet 6 inches per 100 feet	= 343.2 feet per mile
2¼ per cent. or 2 feet 3 inches per 100 feet	= 118.8 feet per mile	6¾ per cent. or 6 feet 9 inches per 100 feet	= 356.4 feet per mile
2½ per cent. or 2 feet 6 inches per 100 feet	= 132.0 feet per mile	7 per cent. or 7 feet 0 inches per 100 feet	= 369.6 feet per mile
2¾ per cent. or 2 feet 9 inches per 100 feet	= 145.2 feet per mile	7½ per cent. or 7 feet 6 inches per 100 feet	= 396.0 feet per mile
3 per cent. or 3 feet 0 inches per 100 feet	= 158.4 feet per mile	8 per cent. or 8 feet 0 inches per 100 feet	= 422.4 feet per mile
3¼ per cent. or 3 feet 3 inches per 100 feet	= 171.6 feet per mile	8½ per cent. or 8 feet 6 inches per 100 feet	= 448.8 feet per mile
3½ per cent. or 3 feet 6 inches per 100 feet	= 184.8 feet per mile	9 per cent. or 9 feet 0 inches per 100 feet	= 475.2 feet per mile
3¾ per cent. or 3 feet 9 inches per 100 feet	= 198.0 feet per mile	9½ per cent. or 9 feet 6 inches per 100 feet	= 501.6 feet per mile
4 per cent. or 4 feet 0 inches per 100 feet	= 211.2 feet per mile	10 per cent. or 10 feet 0 inches per 100 feet	= 528.0 feet per mile
4¼ per cent. or 4 feet 3 inches per 100 feet	= 224.4 feet per mile		

ESTIMATED AMOUNT OF MATERIAL REQUIRED FOR ONE MILE OF TRACK WHEN VARIOUS WEIGHT RAIL IS USED

Weight of Rails per yard	16	20	25	30	35	40	45	50	55	60	65	70	75	80	85	90	95	100
Number of tons of Rails 2,240 pounds	25	31½	39¼	47	55	63	70¾	78½	86½	94¼	102	110	117¾	125½	133¼	141½	149½	157
Pounds of Spikes . . .	1805	3406	3770	3770	4140	4512	6212	6420	6420	6420	6420	6420	6420	6420	6420	6420	6420	6420
Number of Splice Joints	374	374	374	374	374	374	374	374	374	374	374	374	374	374	374	374	374	374
Number of Cross-Ties .	3520	3520	3520	3520	3017	3017	2640	2640	2640	2640	2348	2348	2348	2348	2113	2113	2113	2113
Pounds of Bolts and Nuts	318	335	353	764	764	1124	1124	1171	1217	1825	1893	1896	1966	1966	2035	2035	2035	2104
Number of Lock Nuts .	1496	1496	1496	1496	1496	1496	1496	1496	1496	2244	2244	2244	2244	2244	2244	2244	2244	2244

On account of fluctuation in price of material, also the variation of price of such material required in different localities, we will not endeavor to give estimate of cost of one mile of track for each weight of rail. However, having prices of various material and using amount required as given in above table, a quick estimate can be made for any weight rail.

APPROXIMATE WEIGHTS OF INDUSTRIAL CARS

Common Name	Light Weight	Capacity	Gauge	Common Name	Light Weight	Capacity	Gauge
	Lbs.	Lbs.			Lbs.	Lbs.	
Contractors — 1 cubic yard . . .	1400	3000	36	Colliery Cars — 40 bushels	1250	3000	36–44
Contractors — 1½ cubic yards . .	2100	4500	36	Colliery Cars — 46 bushels	1400	3500	36–44
Contractors — 2 cubic yards . .	2500	6000	36	Colliery Cars — 54 bushels	1700	4100	36–44
Contractors — 2½ cubic yards . .	3000	7500	36	Colliery Cars — 2½ long tons	2000	5700	36–44
Contractors — 3 cubic yards . .	4000	9000	36	Colliery Cars — 3 long tons	2500	6700	36–44
Contractors — 4 cubic yards . .	5000	12000	36	Logging Cars — 4-wheel .	3000	1000 ft.	36–56½
Colliery Cars — 15 bushels . . .	500	1200	36–44	Logging Cars — 4-wheel .	5000	2000 ft.	36–56½
Colliery Cars — 20 bushels . . .	600	1500	36–44	Logging Cars — 4-wheel .	6000	2500 ft.	36–56½
Colliery Cars — 25 bushels . . .	850	1900	36–44	Logging Cars — 8-wheel .	6900	2000 to 2500 ft.	36–56½
Colliery Cars — 30 bushels . . .	950	2300	36–44	Logging Cars — 8-wheel .	8400	3000 to 3500 ft.	36–56½
Colliery Cars — 33 bushels . . .	1050	2500	36–44	Logging Cars — 8-wheel .	9600	4000 to 4500 ft.	36–56½
Colliery Cars — 35 bushels . . .	1150	2700	36–44	Logging Cars — 8-wheel .	11000	5000 ft.	36–56½

WEIGHTS OF VARIOUS MATERIALS

Material	Weight — Pounds	Material	Weight — Pounds
Water — 1 gallon U. S. standard, 231 cubic inches	8⅓	Coal — Average per cubic foot, anthracite	54
Water — 1 gallon Imperial, 277¼ cubic inches . .	10	Note. — Average bulk of one ton coal (2240 lbs.), bituminous, 43 cubic feet; anthracite, 41.5 cubic feet.	
Gravel — 1 cubic foot	125		
Gravel — 1 cubic yard	3350	Lumber — Board measure per 1,000 feet —	
Sand — 1 cubic yard	3000 to 3500	Yellow or Norway pine	3000 to 4500
Clay — 1 cubic yard	2200 to 2600	White pine	2500 to 4000
Rock — 1 cubic yard (broken)	2600 to 3000	Logs — Green, per 1,000 feet (yellow pine, Norway pine,	
Coal — Average per cubic foot, bituminous . . .	52	white pine, or hemlock)	8000 to 10000

SHIPMENT OF LOCOMOTIVES

All sizes of locomotives, up to and including 36 tons, are shipped on flat cars, set-up ready for fuel, water and firing-up for service. Locomotives over 36 tons, when built for standard gauge track, are shipped on their own wheels. Shay locomotives of narrow or unusual gauge, when weighing over 42 tons, are shipped, as a rule, on standard gauge trucks, and the engine trucks loaded on a flat car accompanying locomotive. All small parts liable to injury or theft en route are removed and either secured inside of the cab, which is carefully enclosed, or properly boxed and loaded on a car. All bright work is protected from rust by a specially prepared compound.

70-Ton Shay Locomotive Hauling Train Load of Logs on 12% Grade

Switch Back, Loop Creek Branch Chesapeake & Ohio Railway, 4½% Grade, 150-Ton Shay Pushing Train

EXPORT TRADE

We have been engaged in building locomotives for service in foreign countries for many years and are thoroughly familiar with the requirements. Shay Locomotives are particularly suited to meet the unusual conditions which are encountered in the construction and development of new railroads in rough and mountainous districts. They are the best engines for plantation and mine service and all kinds of development projects.

All of our locomotives are erected complete and given a running test in our shops before being dismantled and packed. The greatest care is used in packing. All bright parts are protected against rust, with a compound. All pieces are tagged and numbered and a packing list furnished with full directions for erecting.

For convenience, each locomotive described in this catalogue has a code word in the line opposite the weight. When one of these words is used we will understand to which locomotive the message refers.

This and following pages show types of locomotives built by
Lima Locomotive Works, Inc.

LIMA SHAY GEARED LOCOMOTIVES

We are equipped to build locomotives of any type and size for either main line or industrial service.

LIMA LOCOMOTIVE WORKS, INCORPORATED
LIMA, OHIO

MEMORANDUM OF CONDITIONS

Gauge of track (i. e., space between the rails)..

Length of haul..Maximum speed..

Weight of rail per yard..Tie spacing center to center....................................

Description of fuel..

Steepest up-grade for loaded cars.............................Length of same.....................................

Must train be started on grade?..

State if cars on return trip are empty..

Steepest up-grade for return trip with empties..

Length of this grade..Radius of sharpest curve..........................

Does curve come on grade?................If so, is grade reduced to equalize resistance of curve?...............

Kind of traffic...

....

Greatest number of cars to be handled per trip..

Weight empty car...Weight loaded car....................................

Style of couplers..Height of couplers from rail.........................

Are there any limitations as to height or width?..
<small>If there are any limitations as to height and width, indicate on diagram on the reverse side of this sheet.</small>

Remarks...

....

....

Send sketch profile of road if possible, showing location of   Signed..
grades and curves, giving length, etc.

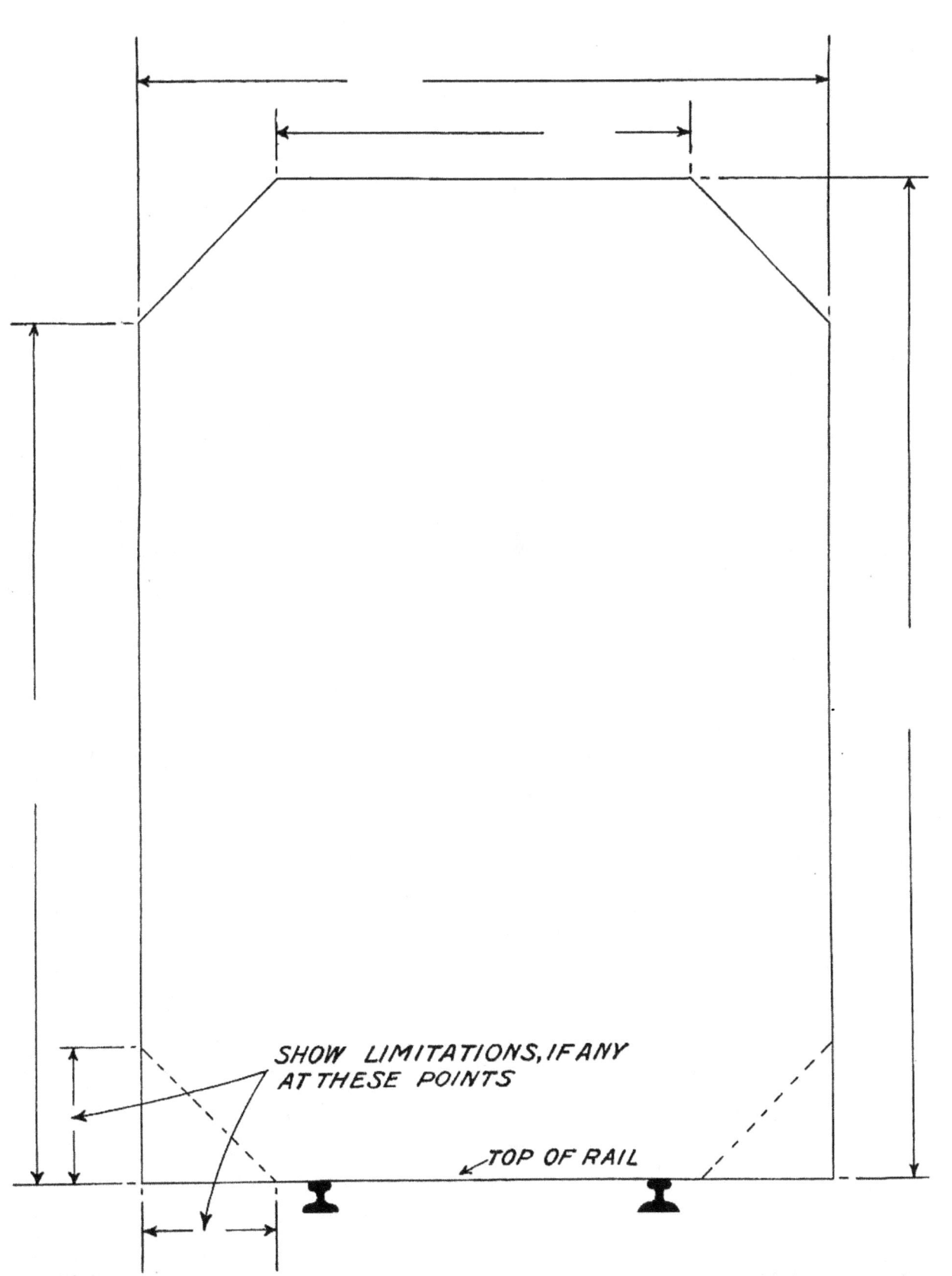

REPAIR PARTS
SHAY GEARED LOCOMOTIVES

CATALOGUE Nº X 2

REPAIR PARTS DEPARTMENT
& WORKS. LIMA, OHIO.

NORTHWESTERN REPRESENTATIVES:
HOFIUS STEEL & EQUIPMENT COMPANY,
L.C. SMITH BUILDING,
SEATTLE, WASHINGTON.

SOUTHWESTERN REPRESENTATIVES:
NORMAN B. LIVERMORE & COMPANY,
1306 MERCHANTS' NATIONAL BANK BLDG.,
SAN FRANCISCO, CALIFORNIA.

MEXICAN REPRESENTATIVES:
INTERNATIONAL RAILWAY SUPPLY COMPANY,
30 CHURCH STREET,
NEW YORK CITY.

CHINESE REPRESENTATIVES:
VIVIAN BOND & COMPANY,
68 BEAVER STREET,
NEW YORK CITY.

GENERAL SALES OFFICES,
17 EAST 42ND STREET,
NEW YORK CITY

SOUTHERN REPRESENTATIVES:
WOODWARD, WIGHT & COMPANY,
NEW ORLEANS,
LOUISIANA.

HAWAIIAN REPRESENTATIVES
THE B. F. DILLINGHAM CO. LTD.,
HONOLULU, T.H.

SOUTH AMERICAN REPRESENTATIVES:
W. R. GRACE & COMPANY,
7 HANOVER SQUARE,
NEW YORK CITY.

JAPANESE REPRESENTATIVES:
TAKATA & COMPANY,
50 CHURCH STREET,
NEW YORK CITY.

CABLE ADDRESS: SHAYLOCO NEW YORK.
CODES. WESTERN UNION, LIEBERS, A.B.C. 5TH. EDITION, MCNEIL'S.

LIMA LOCOMOTIVE WORKS, INCORPORATED, LIMA, OHIO

Lima Locomotive Works, Incorporated, maintains at its plant at Lima, Ohio, a complete Repair Parts Department, the object of which is to furnish promptly repair parts for all locomotives of its manufacture.

A complete stock of repair parts for all sizes of standard Shay Geared Locomotives is maintained, thus permitting immediate shipment of all items requiring renewal and assuring maximum service from all Shay Locomotives.

The purpose in distributing this catalogue is to provide as complete a reference book as possible to assist our customers in placing their orders for Shay repair parts, and to simplify ordering and insure correct understanding of what is wanted.

All Shay parts are manufactured to gauges, jigs or templates, thus insuring the production of standard duplicate parts, and it is only by securing repair parts made at our factory that properly designed details of correct material and workmanship for Shay Geared Locomotives can be obtained.

This catalogue illustrates the various details of Shay Geared Locomotives only. On account of the diversity of design and size of direct connected locomotives it is impossible to prepare a comprehensive repair parts catalogue which would properly cover this field. We are, however, prepared to furnish promptly, repair parts for all direct connected locomotives.

The Repair Parts Department will be glad to co-operate with you in the inspection and overhauling of all classes of locomotives.

CLASS "A"—TWO CYLINDER, TWO TRUCK

CLASS "B"—THREE CYLINDER, TWO TRUCK

CLASS "C"—THREE CYLINDER, THREE TRUCK

CLASS "D"—THREE CYLINDER, FOUR TRUCK

INSTRUCTIONS FOR ORDERING

The following plates illustrate various parts of Shay Locomotives. A key giving the name of the detail will be found on the page opposite or immediately following each plate.

A code word has been assigned to each detail, and when ordering repair parts either by letter, telephone or telegraph, specify the shop number of the locomotive and the code word of the part required.

The illustrations do not, of course, cover the exact design of details for all locomotives. If, however, the shop number of your locomotive and the code word of the detail as shown in this catalogue are given there will be no difficulty in filling the order correctly.

The shop number of the locomotive which should be furnished in all cases will be found on the name plate on the side of the smoke box as shown on Plate No. 6.

Destination and definite shipping instructions—express, parcel post, or freight—should be given in all cases.

In the past some trouble has been experienced on account of changes having been made in older locomotives after shipment from our Works, and of which we have no knowledge.

Our records cover the locomotives as built by us and if changes have been made in any details of your locomotive since shipment from our Works, full information should be given when orders are placed with us for repair parts affected by these changes.

PLATE 1

Cylinder and Cylinder Details

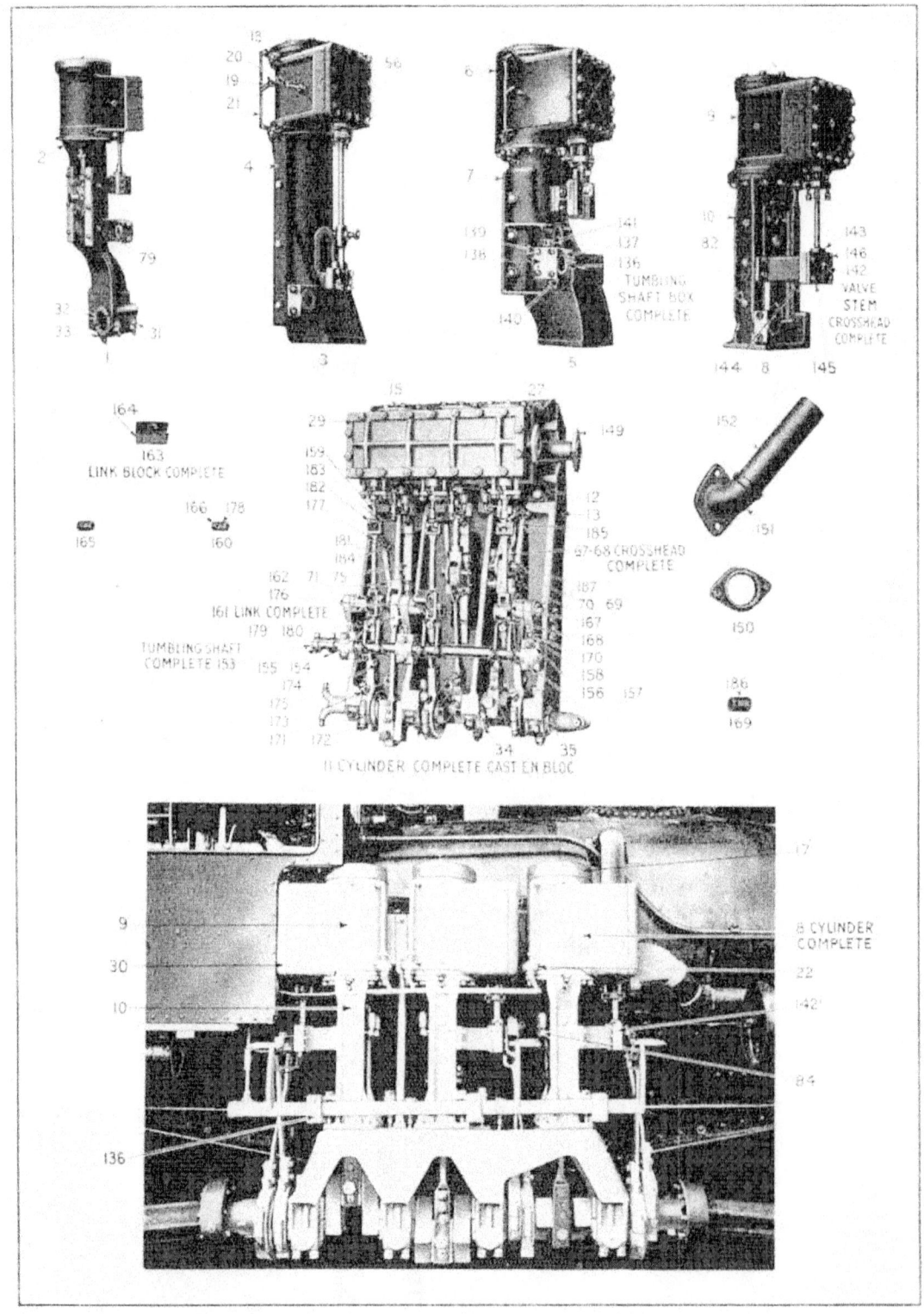

PLATE 2

Cylinder and Cylinder Details

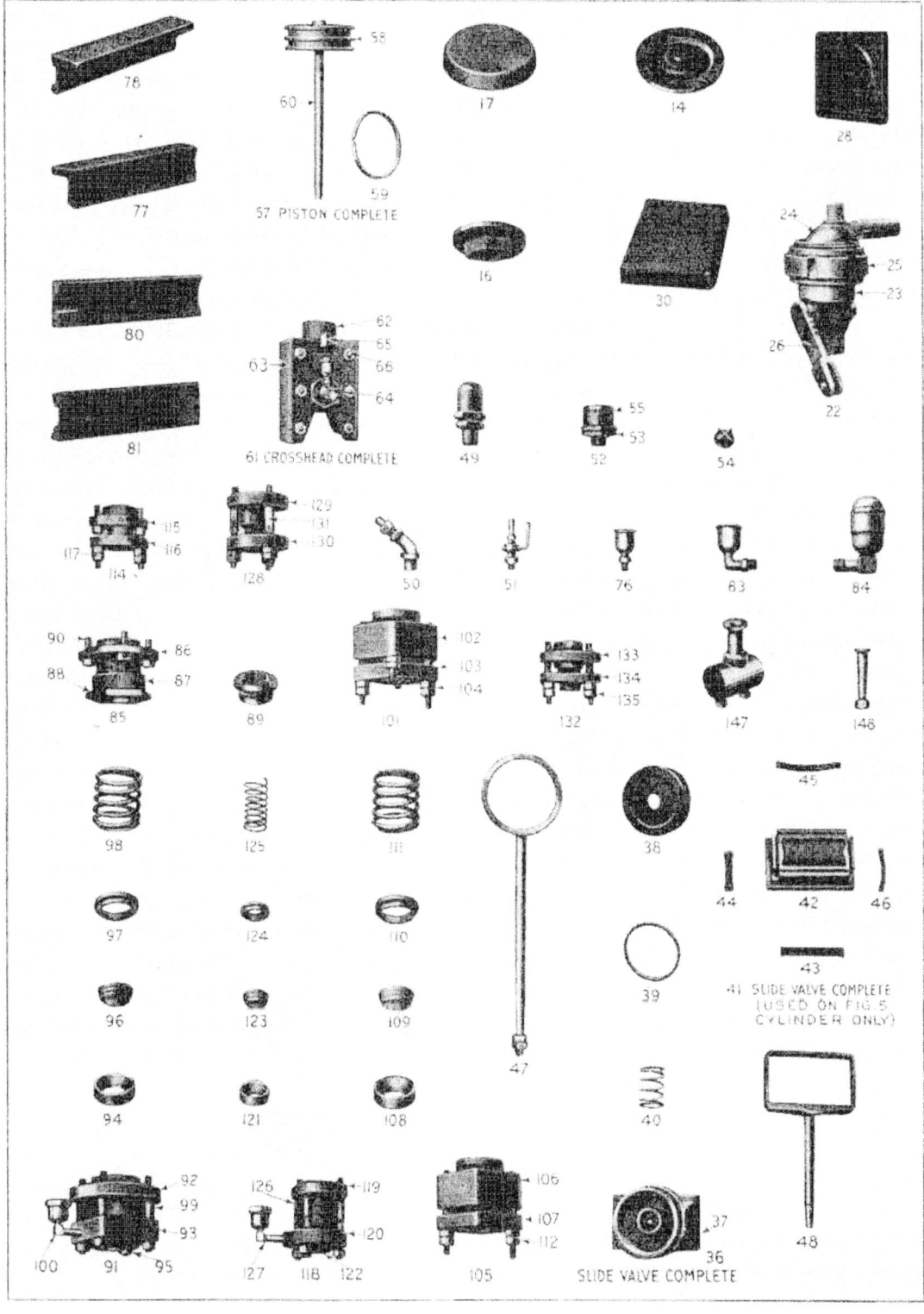

PLATES 1 and 2
Cylinder and Cylinder Details

CODE WORD	FIG.	NAME OF PART
Cabal	1	CYLINDER, COMPLETE
Cackle	2	Cylinder bare
Cage	3	CYLINDER, COMPLETE
Cajole	4	Cylinder bare
Calibre	5	CYLINDER, COMPLETE
Called	6	Cylinder barrel, bare
Callous	7	Cylinder frame, bare
Calm	8	CYLINDER, COMPLETE
Camp	9	Cylinder barrel, bare
Candid	10	Cylinder frame, bare
Canon	11	CYLINDER, COMPLETE, CAST EN BLOC
Capable	12	Cylinder barrel, cast en bloc
Capital	13	Cylinder frame, cast en bloc
Caprice	14	Cylinder head
Carnage	15	Cylinder head top (Used on Fig. 11 cylinder only)
Carol	16	Cylinder head bottom (Used on Fig. 11 cylinder only)
Carp	17	Cylinder head casing
Carpet	18	CYLINDER COCK, COMPLETE
Carry	19	Cylinder cock lever
Cash	20	Cylinder cock eye bolt
Casual	21	Cylinder cock connecting bar
Catch	22	CYLINDER COCK, COMPLETE, TWIN VALVE
Caution	23	Cylinder cock body
Cavil	24	Cylinder cock cap
Cease	25	Cylinder cock nut
Cede	26	Cylinder cock valve handle
Celerity	27	Steam chest (Used on Fig. 11 cylinder only)
Cement	28	Steam chest cover
Censure	29	Steam chest cover (Used on Fig. 11 cylinder only)
Central	30	Steam chest cover casing
Certain	31	Cylinder crank bearing cap—See Note
Certify	32	Cylinder crank bearing brass, top—See Note
Cession	33	Cylinder crank bearing brass, bottom—See Note
Champion	34	Cylinder crank bearing cap (Used on Fig. 11 cylinder only)
Chance	35	Cylinder crank bearing brass, one pair (Used on Fig. 11 cylinder only)
Chaplet	36	SLIDE VALVE, COMPLETE
Charity	37	Slide valve
Charlatan	38	Slide valve balance plate
Chary	39	Slide valve balance plate ring
Chase	40	Slide valve balance plate spring
Chasten	41	SLIDE VALVE, COMPLETE (Used on Fig. 5 cylinder only)
Chat	42	Slide valve (Used on Fig. 5 cylinder only)
Chattels	43	Slide valve balance strip, long (Used on Fig. 5 cylinder only)
Cheap	44	Slide valve balance strip, short (Used on Fig. 5 cylinder only)
Chew	45	Slide valve balance spring, long (Used on Fig. 5 cylinder only)
Chide	46	Slide valve balance spring, short (Used on Fig. 5 cylinder only)
Choler	47	Valve yoke
Chuckle	48	Valve yoke (Used on Fig. 5 cylinders only)
Churlish	49	STEAM CHEST RELIEF VALVE, COMPLETE
Cipher	50	STEAM CHEST OIL PIPE ELBOW, COMPLETE
Citadel	51	STEAM CHEST DRAIN COCK, COMPLETE
Cite	52	STEAM CHEST RELIEF VALVE, COMPLETE (Used on Fig. 5 cylinder only)
Civic	53	Steam chest relief valve seat (Used on Fig. 5 cylinders only)
Clasp	54	Steam chest relief valve (Used on Fig. 5 cylinders only)
Clause	55	Steam chest relief valve cap (Used on Fig. 5 cylinders only)
Cleave	56	Steam chest cover studs
Clemency	57	PISTON COMPLETE
Clever	58	Piston head
Climate	59	Piston packing rings
Climb	60	Piston rod and nut
Clothes	61	CROSSHEAD COMPLETE
Cloudy	62	Crosshead
Clownish	63	Crosshead shoe
Clumsy	64	Crosshead pin and nut
Cluster	65	Crosshead key
Coadjutor	66	Crosshead shoe bolts
Coalesce	67	CROSSHEAD COMPLETE (Used on Fig. 11 cylinder only)
Coalition	68	Crosshead (Used on Fig. 11 cylinder only)

PLATES 1 and 2—(Continued)

CODE WORD	FIG.	NAME OF PART
Cockney	69	Crosshead shoe (Used on Fig. 11 cylinder only)
Coddle	70	Crosshead pin and nut (Used on Fig. 11 cylinder only)
Codger	71	Crosshead key (Used on Fig. 11 cylinder only)
Codify	72	Crosshead liner, thick (Used on Fig. 11 cylinder only) (No illustration)
Coerce	73	Crosshead liner, thin (Used on Fig. 11 cylinder only) (No illustration)
Coeval	74	Crosshead side plate (Used on Fig. 11 cylinder only) (No illustration)
Coexist	75	Crosshead guide—with bolts (Used on Fig. 11 cylinder only)
Cogent	76	Crosshead pin oil cup
Cogitate	77	Crosshead guide — outside (Used on Fig. 1 cylinder only)
Cohere	78	Crosshead guide — inside (Used on Fig. 1 cylinder only)
Cohibit	79	Crosshead guide set screws (Used on Fig. 1 cylinder only)
Coincide	80	Crosshead guide—outside
Collision	81	Crosshead guide—inside
Collocate	82	Crosshead guide bolts
Colloquy	83	Crosshead guide oil cup (Used on Fig. 1-3 cylinders)
Color	84	Crosshead guide oil cup (Used on Fig. 5-8 cylinders)
Colossal	85	PISTON ROD PACKING COMPLETE — FIBRE
Combat	86	Stuffing box
Comely	87	Stuffing box gland
Comic	88	Stuffing box nut
Comity	89	Follower
Companion	90	Studs
Compeer	91	PISTON ROD PACKING COMPLETE — METALLIC
Compel	92	Stuffing box
Compete	93	Stuffing box gland
Competitor	94	Vibrating cup— See Note
Comply	95	Swab cup
Component	96	Packing rings—See Note
Comport	97	Spring washer top
Composure	98	Spring
Compress	99	Packing studs
Comprise	100	Packing oil cup
Compute	101	PISTON ROD PACKING COMPLETE— FIBRE
Comrade	102	Stuffing box
Concave	103	Stuffing box gland
Conceal	104	Studs
Concede	105	PISTON ROD PACKING COMPLETE — METALLIC (Used on Fig. 11 cylinders only)
Conceit	106	Stuffing box (Used on Fig. 11 cylinders only)
Conceive	107	Stuffing box gland (Used on Fig. 11 cylinders only)
Concern	108	Vibrating cup — See Note (Used on Fig. 11 cylinders only)
Concise	109	Packing rings — See Note (Used on Fig. 11 cylinders only)
Conclave	110	Spring washer, top (Used on Fig. 11 cylinders only)
Conclude	111	Spring (Used on Fig. 11 cylinders only)
Concoct	112	Packing studs (Used on Fig. 11 cylinders only)
Concord	113	Packing oil cup (Same as Fig. 100) (Used on Fig. 11 cylinders only)
Concrete	114	VALVE STEM PACKING COMPLETE—FIBRE
Concur	115	Stuffing box
Condemn	116	Stuffing box gland
Condign	117	Studs
Condiment	118	VALVE STEM PACKING COMPLETE — METALLIC
Condole	119	Stuffing box
Conduce	120	Stuffing box gland
Confer	121	Vibrating cup—See Note
Confess	122	Swab cup
Confide	123	Packing rings—See Note
Confine	124	Spring washer top
Confirm	125	Spring
Conflict	126	Studs
Conform	127	Packing oil cup
Confound	128	VALVE STEM PACKING COMPLETE—FIBRE
Confront	129	Stuffing box
Confuse	130	Stuffing box gland
Confute	131	Studs
Congeal	132	VALVE STEM PACKING COMPLETE—FIBRE (Used on Fig. 11 cylinders only)
Congress	133	Stuffing box (Used on Fig. 11 cylinders only)
Conjoin	134	Stuffing box gland (Used on Fig. 11 cylinders only)
Conjure	135	Studs (Used on Fig. 11 cylinders only)

PLATES 1 and 2—(Continued)

CODE WORD	FIG.	NAME OF PART
Connive	136	TUMBLING SHAFT BOX COMPLETE
Conquer	137	Tumbling shaft box
Conquest	138	Tumbling shaft box cap
Console	139	Tumbling shaft box cap tap bolts
Consort	140	Tumbling shaft box tap bolts
Conspire	141	Tumbling shaft box oil cup
Constrain	142	VALVE STEM CROSS HEAD COMPLETE
Contemn	143	Valve stem crosshead
Context	144	Valve stem crosshead stand
Contour	145	Valve stem crosshead stand plate
Contrive	146	Valve stem crosshead stand tap bolts
Contumacy	147	Link block pin for valve stem
Contumely	148	Link block pin for valve stem crosshead
Convene	149	Exhaust manifold (Used on Fig. 11 cylinders only)
Converge	150	Exhaust pipe gland (Used with Fig. 11 cylinders only)
Converse	151	Steam pipe flanged elbow (Used with Fig. 11 cylinders only)
Convivial	152	Steam pipe nipple (Used with Fig. 11 cylinders only)
Convocate	153	TUMBLING SHAFT COMPLETE (Used on Fig. 11 cylinder only)
Convoke	154	Tumbling shaft arms, right (Used on Fig. 11 cylinder only)
Convoy	155	Tumbling shaft arms, left (Used on Fig. 11 cylinder only)
Convulse	156	Tumbling shaft box cap (Used on Fig. 11 cylinder only)
Coop	157	Tumbling shaft box cap tap bolts (Used on Fig. 11 cylinder only)
Cope	158	Tumbling shaft box oil cup (Used on Fig. 11 cylinder only)
Copious	159	Valve stem connection (Used on Fig. 11 cylinders only)
Core	160	Valve stem connection bushing (Used on Fig. 11 cylinders only)
Corner	161	LINK COMPLETE (Used on Fig. 11 cylinder only)
Cornice	162	Link (Used on Fig. 11 cylinder only)
Corollary	163	LINK BLOCK COMPLETE (Used on Fig. 11 cylinder only)
Corpulent	164	Link block (Used on Fig. 11 cylinder only)
Corpuscle	165	Link block bushing (Used on Fig. 11 cylinder only)
Corrode	166	Link bushings (Used on Fig. 11 cylinder only)
Corrupt	167	Link saddles (Used on Fig. 11 cylinder only)
Cosmical	168	Link saddle bolts (Used on Fig. 11 cylinder only)
Coverlet	169	Link saddle bushing (Used on Fig. 11 cylinder only)
Covet	170	Link hanger bracket (Used on Fig. 11 cylinder only)
Cower	171	ECCENTRIC STRAP COMPLETE—See Note (Used on Fig. 11 cylinder only)
Coxcomb	172	Eccentric strap bolts (Used on Fig. 11 cylinder only)
Cozen	173	Eccentric strap oil cup (Used on Fig. 11 cylinder only)
Crabbed	174	Eccentric blades (Used on Fig. 11 cylinder only)
Crave	175	Eccentric blade bolts (Used on Fig. 11 cylinder only)
Credence	176	Eccentric blade pin (Used on Fig. 11 cylinder only)
Crest	177	Link radius rod with bushings (Used on Fig. 11 cylinder only)
Crimp	178	Link radius rod bushing (Used on Fig. 11 cylinder only)
Cringe	179	Link radius rod guide (Used on Fig. 11 cylinder only)
Crone	180	Link radius rod pin (Used on Fig. 11 cylinder only)
Crude	181	Combination lever (Used on Fig. 11 cylinder only)
Cupidity	182	Combination lever valve connection pin (Used on Fig. 11 cylinder only)
Cursory	183	Combination lever radius rod pin (Used on Fig. 11 cylinder only)

PLATES 1 and 2—(Continued)

CODE WORD	FIG.	NAME OF PART	CODE WORD	FIG.	NAME OF PART
Curtail	184	Combination lever union link pin (Used on Fig. 11 cylinder only)	*Custody*	186	Union link bushings (Used on Fig. 11 cylinder only)
Curve	185	Union link with bushings (Used on Fig. 11 cylinder only)	*Cynical*	187	Union link bolt (Used on Fig. 11 cylinder only)

NOTE.—When ordering cylinders specify whether front, middle or rear cylinder is required. When ordering cylinder details specify whether wanted for front, middle or rear cylinder.

Eccentric strap is only furnished complete, it being impracticable to furnish top or bottom half separate, due to inability to furnish new half to fit with old.

When ordering packing rings or vibrating cups give diameter of piston rod or valve stem.

When ordering cylinder crank bearing cap for Fig. 1 cylinder, state whether cap is for babbitted bearing or for shell brass.

All orders must specify the SHOP NUMBER of locomotive and the "CODE WORD" of the part required.

In preparing order, read over instructions for ordering carefully to see that you have covered all that is needed to enable us to fill order.

PLATE 3

Valve Motion and Details

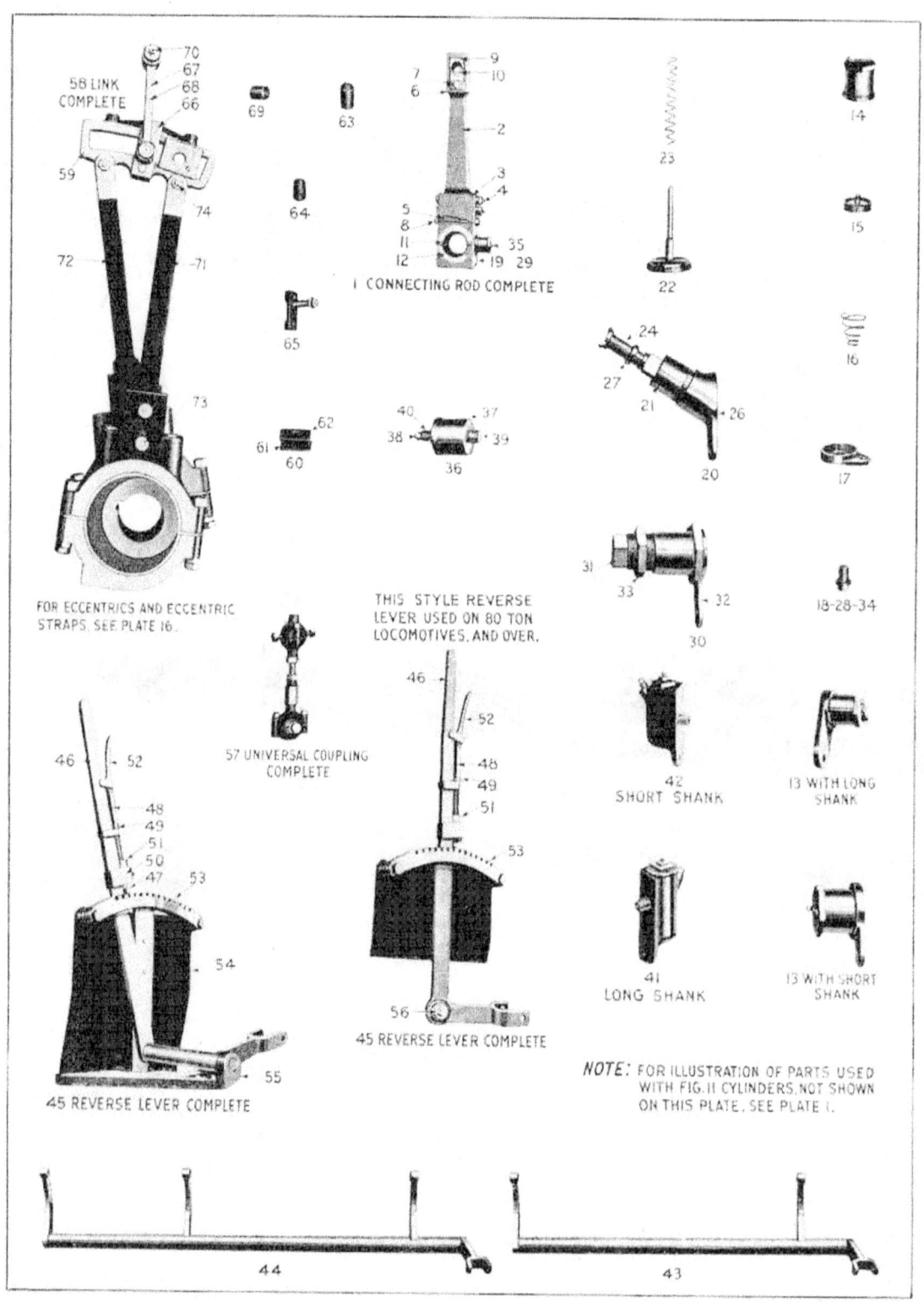

PLATE 3

Valve Motion and Details

CODE WORD	FIG.	NAME OF PART
Vacancy	1	CONNECTING ROD COMPLETE
Vacant	2	Connecting rod stub
Vacate	3	Connecting rod strap
Vacation	4	Connecting rod strap bolts
Vacillate	5	Connecting rod wedge, crank end
Vacuity	6	Connecting rod wedge, crosshead end
Vagary	7	Connecting rod wedge bolt, crosshead end
Vagrant	8	Connecting rod wedge bolt, crank end
Vague	9	Connecting rod crosshead pin, brass, top
Vain	10	Connecting rod crosshead pin, brass, bottom
Valient	11	Connecting rod crank pin, brass, top—See Note
Valor	12	Connecting rod crank pin, brass, bottom—See Note
Vanish	13	CONNECTING ROD GREASE CUP COMPLETE—See Note
Vanity	14	Grease cup chamber
Vanquish	15	Grease cup piston
Vapid	16	Grease cup piston spring
Vapor	17	Grease cup base
Variable	18	Grease cup screw plug
Variety	19	Grease cup tap screw
Various	20	ANGLE GREASE CUP COMPLETE
Varnish	21	Angle grease cup chamber
Vary	22	Angle grease cup piston
Vast	23	Angle grease cup spring
Vaunt	24	Angle grease cup spring follower
Veer	26	Angle grease cup base
Vegetate	27	Angle grease cup lock nut
Veil	28	Angle grease cup screw plug
Velocity	29	Angle grease cup tap screw
Vend	30	PLUG GREASE CUP COMPLETE
Venerate	31	Plug grease cup plug
Venial	32	Plug grease cup base
Venom	33	Plug grease cup lock nut
Vent	34	Plug grease cup screw plug
Venture	35	Plug grease cup tap screw
Veracity	36	GREASE CUP COMPLETE
Verge	37	Grease cup chamber
Verily	38	Grease cup piston
Vernal	39	Grease cup screw plug
Versed	40	Grease cup lock nut
Version	41	NEEDLE VALVE OIL CUP COMPLETE Long shank
Vestige	42	NEEDLE VALVE OIL CUP COMPLETE Short shank
Veteran	43	Tumbling shaft, two cylinder locomotive
Vexation	44	Tumbling shaft, three cylinder locomotive
Vibrate	45	REVERSE LEVER COMPLETE
Vicious	46	Reverse lever
Victim	47	Reverse lever latch
Victory	48	Reverse lever latch lifter
Victuals	49	Reverse lever latch stem
View	50	Reverse lever latch stem guide
Vigilant	51	Reverse lever latch gib
Vilify	52	Reverse lever handle
Villain	53	Reverse lever quadrant
Violate	54	Reverse lever quadrant plate
Violence	55	Reverse lever shaft stand
Violent	56	Reverse lever pin, nut and washer
Virago	57	UNIVERSAL COUPLING COMPLETE
Virgin	58	LINK COMPLETE
Virile	59	Link
Virtue	60	Link block complete
Viscid	61	Link block
Visible	62	Link block plates
Vision	63	Link block bushing
Vital	64	Link bushings
Vitiate	65	Link saddle
Vivid	66	Link saddle bolts
		Link block pin for valve stem (See Plate 2, Fig. 147)
		Link block pin for valve stem crosshead (See Plate 2, Fig. 148)
Voice	67	LINK HANGER COMPLETE
Volatile	68	Link hanger

(Continued on Page 16)

PLATE 4

Steam and Bottom Brackets

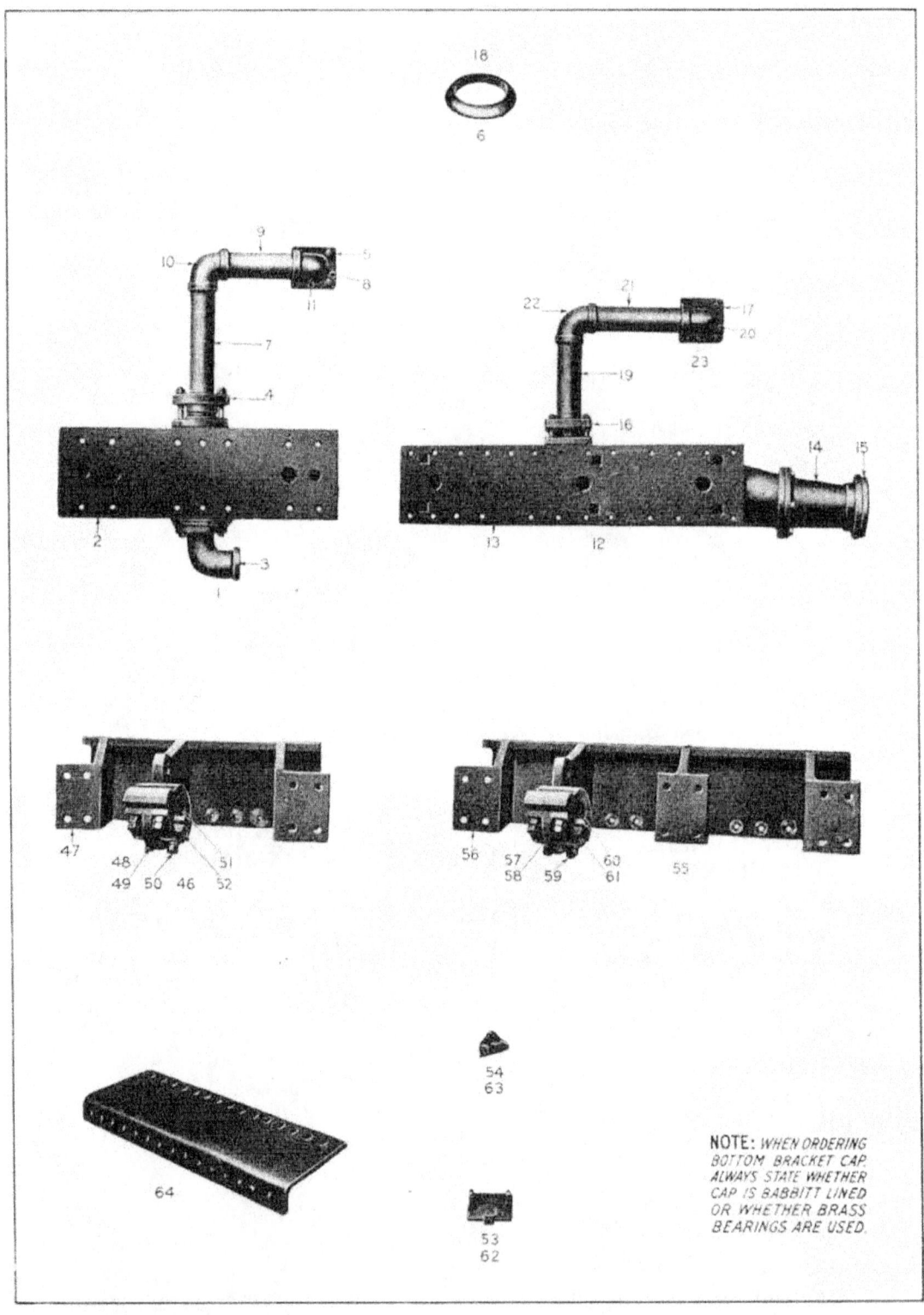

PLATE 5

Steam and Bottom Brackets

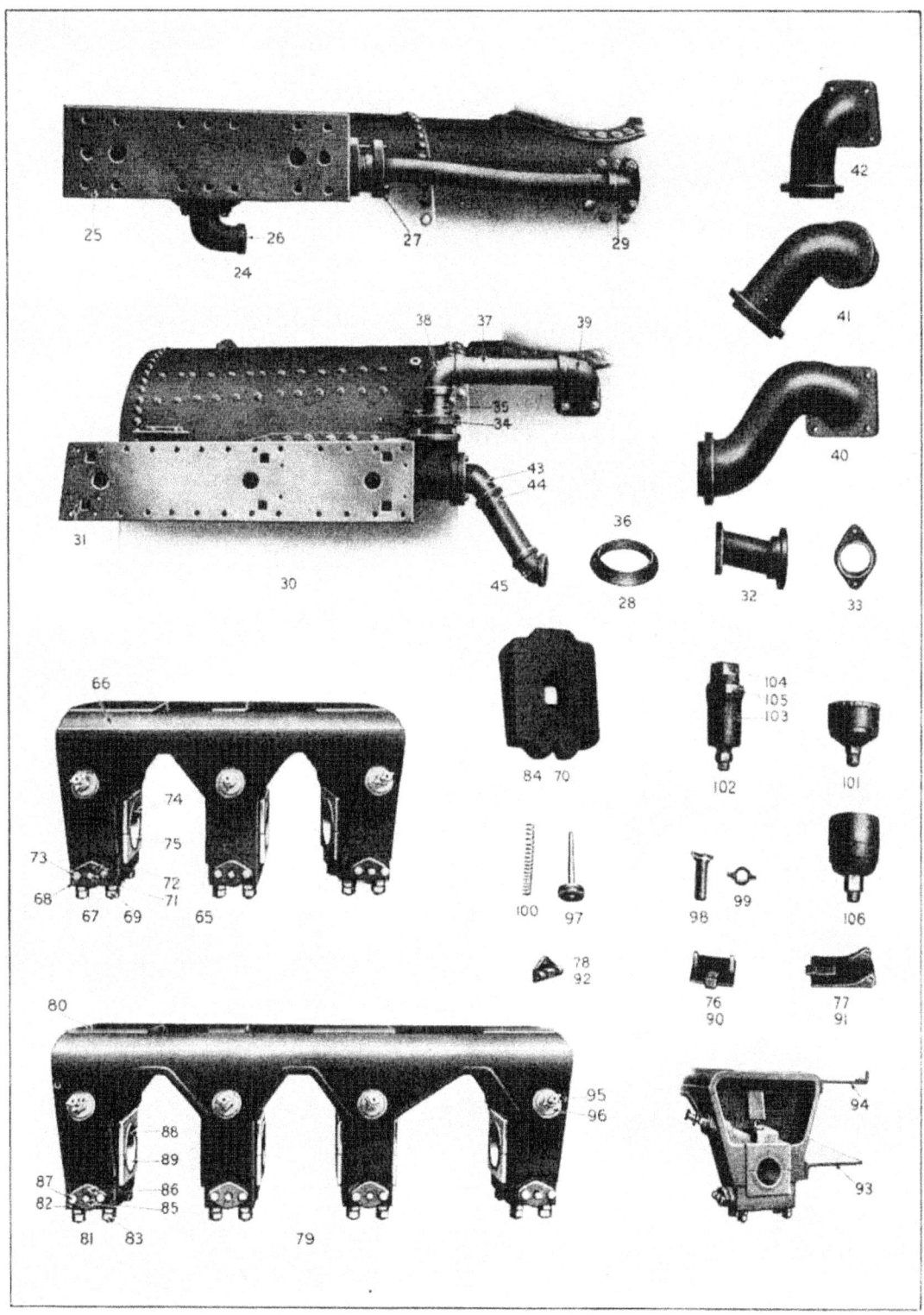

PLATE 3—(Continued)

CODE WORD	FIG.	NAME OF PART	CODE WORD	FIG.	NAME OF PART
Volition	69	Link hanger bushing	Volute	71	Eccentric blades, forward motion
Voluble	70	Link hanger pin	Vorant	72	Eccentric blades, backward motion
		Eccentric strap complete for Fig. 1—3—5—8 cylinders —See Plate 16	Vortex	73	Eccentric blade bolts
		Eccentric strap bolts—See Plate 16	Votary	74	Eccentric blade pin

NOTE.—When ordering connecting rod crank pin brasses, give diameter of crank pin.

Eccentric straps are only furnished in pairs, it being impracticable to furnish top or bottom half separate, due to inability to machine new half to fit with old half.

When ordering oil cup Fig. 13 complete, specify whether long or short shank is wanted.

For Valve Motion Parts for Cylinder, Fig. 11—See Plate 1.

All orders must specify the SHOP NUMBER of locomotive and the "CODE WORD" of the part wanted.

In preparing order, read over instructions for ordering carefully to see that you have covered all that is needed to enable us to fill order.

PLATES 4 and 5

Steam and Bottom Brackets

CODE WORD	FIG.	NAME OF PART	CODE WORD	FIG.	NAME OF PART
Sable	1	STEAM BRACKET COMPLETE, two cylinder locomotive	Scene	27	Steam pipe gland, at bracket
			Sceptic	28	Steam pipe joint ring
			Schism	29	Steam pipe elbow
Sack	2	Steam bracket, bare	Scion	30	STEAM BRACKET COMPLETE, three cylinder locomotive
Sacred	3	Exhaust elbow			
Sage	4	Steam pipe gland at bracket			
Sailor	5	Steam pipe gland at boiler			
Saintly	6	Steam pipe joint ring	Scoff	31	Steam bracket bare
Sake	7	Steam pipe nipple at bracket	Scold	32	Exhaust reducer
Salient	8	Steam pipe nipple at boiler	Scour	33	Exhaust reducer gland
Sally	9	Steam pipe nipple plain	Scowl	34	Steam pipe gland, at bracket
Salute	10	Steam pipe elbow, plain	Scraggy	35	Steam pipe nipple, at bracket
Salve	11	Steam pipe elbow, plain	Scrape	36	Steam pipe joint ring
Same	12	STEAM BRACKET COMPLETE, three cylinder locomotive	Scream	37	Steam pipe nipple, plain
			Screen	38	Steam pipe elbow, plain
			Secede	39	Steam pipe flange elbow
Sanative	13	Steam bracket bare	Sedate	40	Steam pipe flange elbow
Sanctify	14	Exhaust reducer	Seduce	41	Steam pipe flange elbow
Sanity	15	Exhaust reducer gland	Seed	42	Steam pipe flange elbow
Sapid	16	Steam pipe gland, at bracket	Seem	43	Exhaust reducer
Sapient	17	Steam pipe gland, at boiler	Segment	44	Exhaust nipple (short)
Satanic	18	Steam pipe joint ring	Seize	45	Exhaust elbow
Sate	19	Steam pipe nipple, at bracket			
Satiate	20	Steam pipe nipple, at boiler			
Savory	21	Steam pipe nipple, plain			
Scant	22	Steam pipe elbow, plain			
Scar	23	Steam pipe elbow, plain			
Scarce	24	STEAM BRACKET COMPLETE, two cylinder locomotive	Seldom	46	BOTTOM BRACKET COMPLETE, two cylinder locomotive
Scarify	25	Steam bracket bare	Select	47	Bottom bracket bare
Scatter	26	Exhaust elbow			

NOTE.—There are several designs of steam pipe flange elbows, Figs. 39, 40, 41, 42 being designs most extensively used. Only one used on locomotive, give number of style corresponding to design of your locomotive.

LIMA LOCOMOTIVE WORKS, INCORPORATED

PLATES 4 and 5—(Continued)

CODE WORD	FIG.	NAME OF PART	CODE WORD	FIG.	NAME OF PART
Selfish	48	BOTTOM BRACKET CAP, COMPLETE, two cylinder locomotive	Sneak	77	Oil cup cover, large
			Snub	78	Oil cup cover hinge lug
			Soar	79	BOTTOM BRACKET COMPLETE, three cylinder locomotive
Sentinel	49	Bottom bracket cap			
Sequel	50	Bottom bracket cap bolts			
Seraphic	51	Crank bearing brass, top	Sober	80	Bottom bracket bare
Serene	52	Crank bearing brass, bottom	Social	81	BOTTOM BRACKET CAP COMPLETE, three cylinder locomotive
Serf	53	Oil cup cover, small			
Servile	54	Oil cup cover hinge lug			
Sever	55	BOTTOM BRACKET COMPLETE, three cylinder locomotive	Soil	82	Bottom bracket cap
			Sojourn	83	Bottom bracket cap bolts
			Solace	84	Bottom bracket cap wedge
Shabby	56	Bottom bracket bare	Sole	85	Bottom bracket cap wedge bolts
Sham	57	BOTTOM BRACKET CAP COMPLETE, three cylinder locomotive			
			Solemn	86	Bottom bracket wedge bolt plate
			Solicit	87	Bottom bracket wedge bolt plate tap bolts
Sheer	58	Bottom bracket cap			
Shine	59	Bottom bracket cap bolts			
Shore	60	Crank bearing brass, top	Solid	88	Crank bearing, top
Shout	61	Crank bearing brass, bottom	Soluble	89	Crank bearing, bottom
Shred	62	Oil cup cover, small	Solve	90	Oil cup cover, small
Shrew	63	Oil cup cover hinge lug	Sombre	91	Oil cup cover, large
Shrill	64	Expansion plate, two and three cylinder locomotive	Song	92	Oil cup cover hinge lug
			Soothe	93	Expansion plate, bottom
			Sophism	94	Expansion plate, top
Shun	65	BOTTOM BRACKET COMPLETE, two cylinder locomotive	Sorcery	95	GREASE CUP COMPLETE, two and three cylinder locomotive
Skill	66	Bottom bracket bare	Sordid	96	Grease cup cap
Skim	67	BOTTOM BRACKET CAP COMPLETE, two cylinder locomotive	Sore	97	Grease cup piston
			Sorrow	98	Grease cup piston follower
			Sound	99	Grease cup follower nut
Skulk	68	Bottom bracket cap	Sour	100	Grease cup spring
Skirt	69	Bottom bracket cap bolts	Source	101	GREASE CUP COMPLETE, plain
Slough	70	Bottom bracket cap wedge			
Smear	71	Bottom bracket cap wedge bolts	Sow	102	PLUG GREASE CUP COMPLETE, two and three cylinder locomotive
Smell	72	Bottom bracket wedge bolt plate			
			Space	103	Plug grease cup body
Smite	73	Bottom bracket wedge bolt plate tap bolts	Sparse	104	Plug grease cup plug
			Species	105	Plug grease cup lock nut
Smoke	74	Crank bearing, top	Speck	106	BRACKET OIL CUP COMPLETE, two and three cylinder locomotive
Snare	75	Crank bearing, bottom			
Snatch	76	Oil cup cover, small			

NOTE.—All orders must specify the SHOP NUMBER of the locomotive and the "CODE WORD" of the part wanted.

In preparing order, read over instructions for ordering carefully to see that you have covered all that is needed to enable us to fill order.

PLATE 6

Boiler, Boiler Details and Outside Fittings

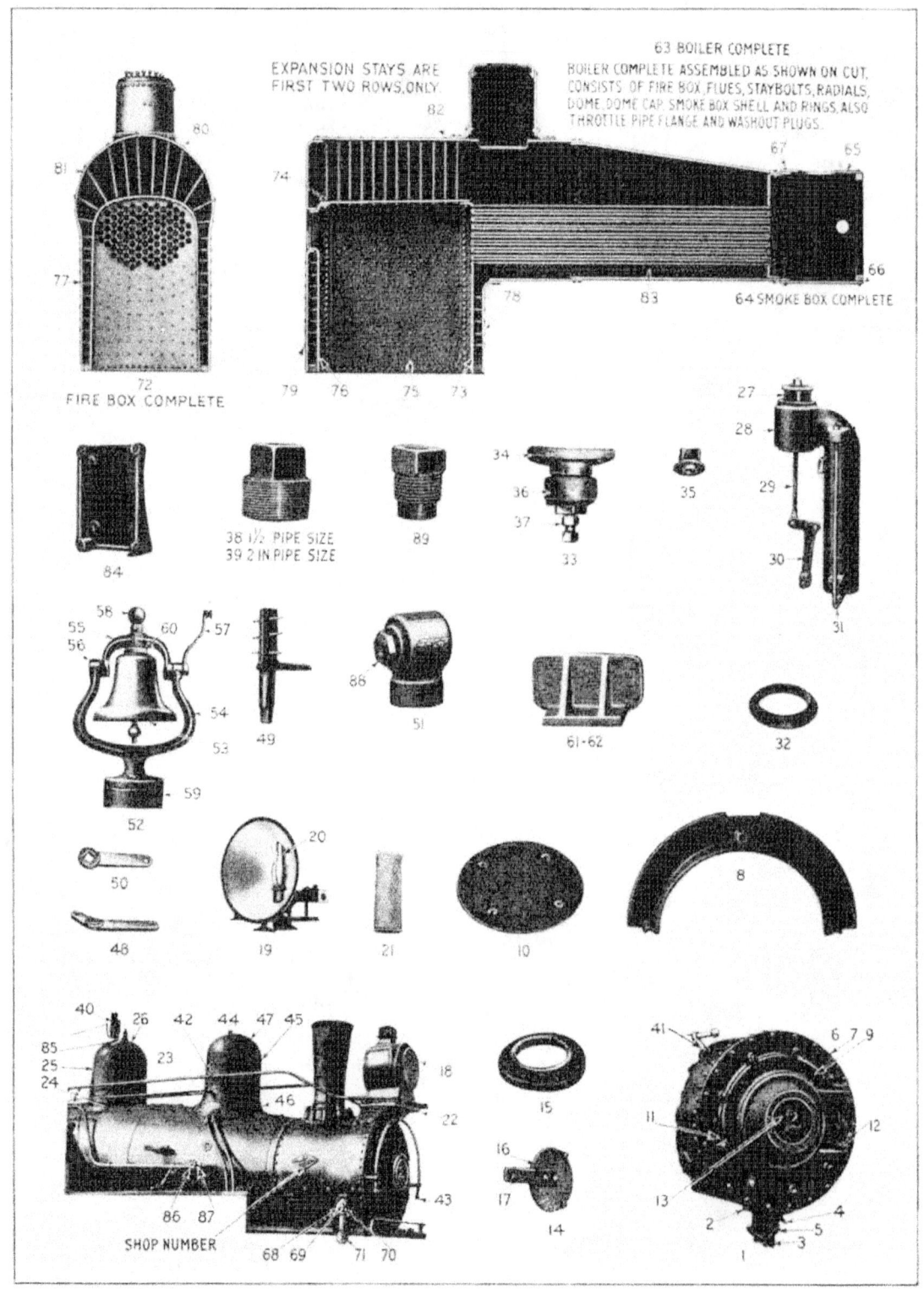

PLATE 6
Boiler, Boiler Details and Outside Fittings

CODE WORD	FIG.	NAME OF PART	CODE WORD	FIG.	NAME OF PART
Babble	1	CINDER POT COMPLETE	Besiege	45	Sand box
Babe	2	Cinder pot base	Besmear	46	Sand box base
Baffle	3	Cinder pot lid	Besotted	47	Sand box cap
Bait	4	Cinder pot hand wheel	Bespeak	48	Sand box lever, long
Balance	5	Cinder pot yoke	Bestead	49	Sand box valve
Balk	6	SMOKE BOX FRONT COMPLETE	Bestir	50	Sand box lever, short
Balmy	7	Smoke box front ring	Betide	51	Air sander
Bandy	8	Smoke box front ring liner	Betimes	52	BELL COMPLETE
Baneful	9	Smoke box front door	Betoken	53	Bell
Banish	10	Smoke box front door liner	Betray	54	Bell frame
Banquet	11	Smoke box front door buttons	Bevy	55	Bell yoke
Banter	12	Smoke box front door hinge pin	Bewail	56	Bell yoke pin
			Beware	57	Bell crank
Barely	13	Number plate	Bewilder	58	Bell knob
Bargain	14	Cleaning hole details complete	Bewitch	59	Bell frame base
			Bias	60	Bell yoke plate
Barren	15	Cleaning hole flange	Bicker	61	Boiler pad, right
Bask	16	Cleaning hole flange cover	Bide	62	Boiler pad, left
Baste	17	Cleaning hole flange cover handle bar	Bigoted	63	BOILER COMPLETE (Consists of firebox, flues, staybolts, radials, dome, dome cap, smokebox shell and rings, also throttle pipe flange and washout plugs)
Battle	18	Headlight			
Bauble	19	Headlight interior			
Basis	20	Headlight chimney	Bind	64	SMOKEBOX COMPLETE
Bawl	21	Headlight wick	Biting	65	Smokebox shell
Bays	22	Headlight bracket	Bitter	66	Smokebox ring, front
Beach	23	DOME CASING COMPLETE	Blacken	67	Smokebox ring, back
			Blade	68	Smoke box brace pad
Beauty	24	Dome casing base	Blanch	69	Smoke box brace bolt
Beck	25	Dome casing shell	Blast	70	Smoke box brace bolt washer
Bedaub	26	Dome casing top	Blatant	71	Smoke box links
Bedeck	27	Throttle valve	Blaze	72	FIREBOX COMPLETE
Bedizen	28	Throttle valve case	Blazon	73	Firebox flue sheet
Befall	29	Throttle valve stem	Bleach	74	Firebox crown sheet
Befitting	30	Throttle bell crank	Blemish	75	Firebox side sheet
Befriend	31	Throttle case yoke	Blench	76	Firebox door sheet
Beggar	32	Throttle pipe joint ring	Blight	77	Staybolts—sides
Beguile	33	WASHOUT VALVE COMPLETE	Blink	78	Staybolts—throat
			Bliss	79	Staybolts—backhead
Behest	34	Washout valve flange	Blithe	80	Radials—crown
Beholder	35	Washout valve	Block	81	Radials—plain
Bellow	36	Washout valve cap	Bloom	82	Radials—expansion
Bend	37	Washout valve cap screw	Bluff	83	Tubes
Benefit	38	1½ in. washout plug	Blunder	84	Air pump bracket
Benison	39	2 in. washout plug	Blush	85	SAFETY VALVES, RIGHT AND LEFT, COMPLETE
Bequeath	40	WHISTLE COMPLETE			
Bereave	41	Hand rail post, long	Boast	86	Check valve
Beseem	42	Hand rail post, short	Bode	87	Stop cock
Beset	43	Hand rail knobs	Bund	88	Air sander nozzle
Beside	44	SAND BOX COMPLETE	Bundle	89	Fusible plug

NOTE.—For throttle lever stem, see Plates 7 and 8 "Inside Cab Fittings, etc."
All orders must specify the SHOP NUMBER of the locomotive and the "CODE WORD" of the part wanted.
Headlight shown is for oil burning; if electric headlight or parts are required specify in your order.
In preparing order, read over instructions for ordering carefully to see that you have covered all that is needed to enable us to fill order.

PLATE 7

Inside Cab Fittings, Smoke Box Arrangement, Ash Pan Details

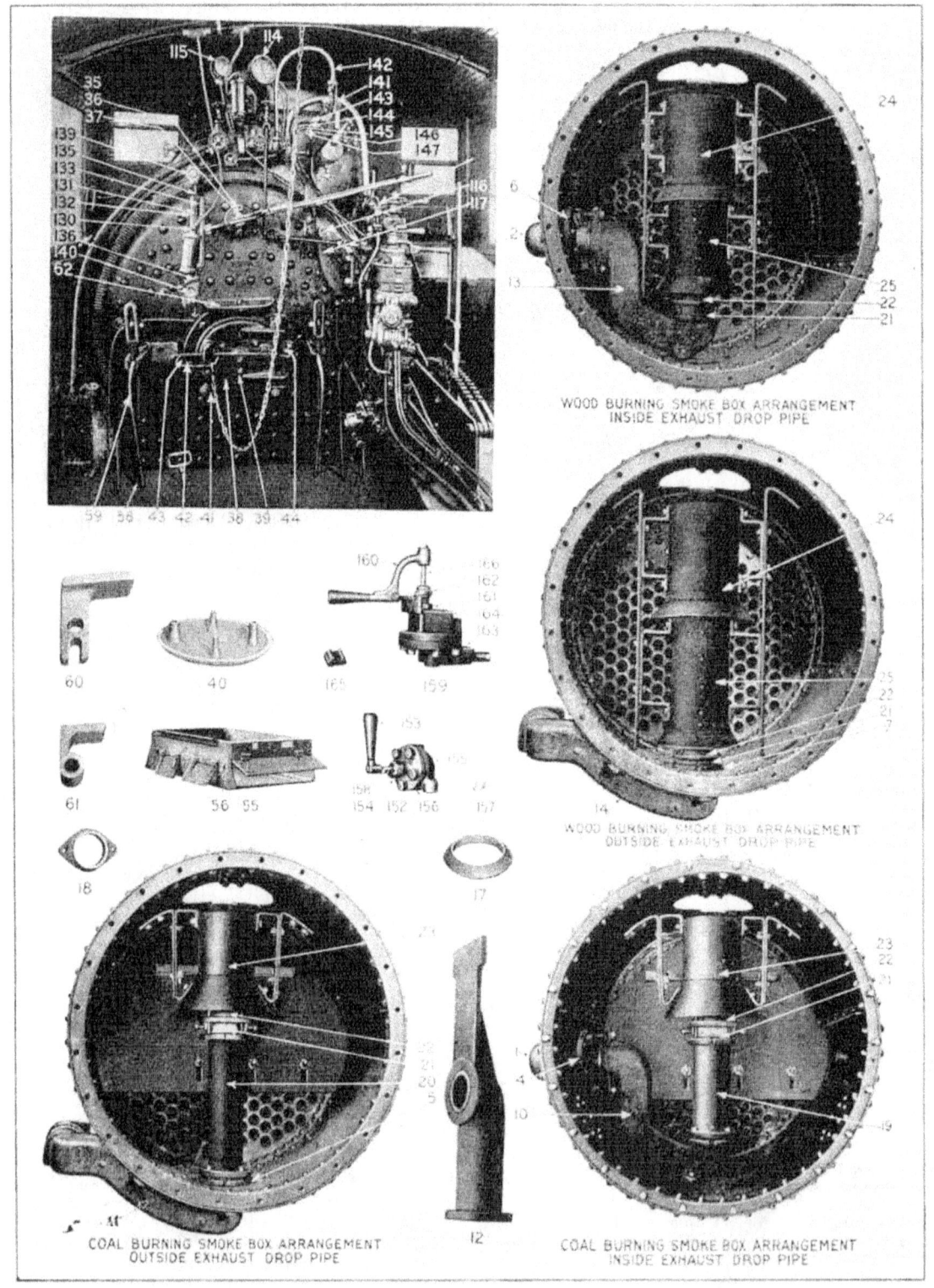

PLATE 8

Inside Cab Fittings, Smoke Box Arrangement, Ash Pan Details

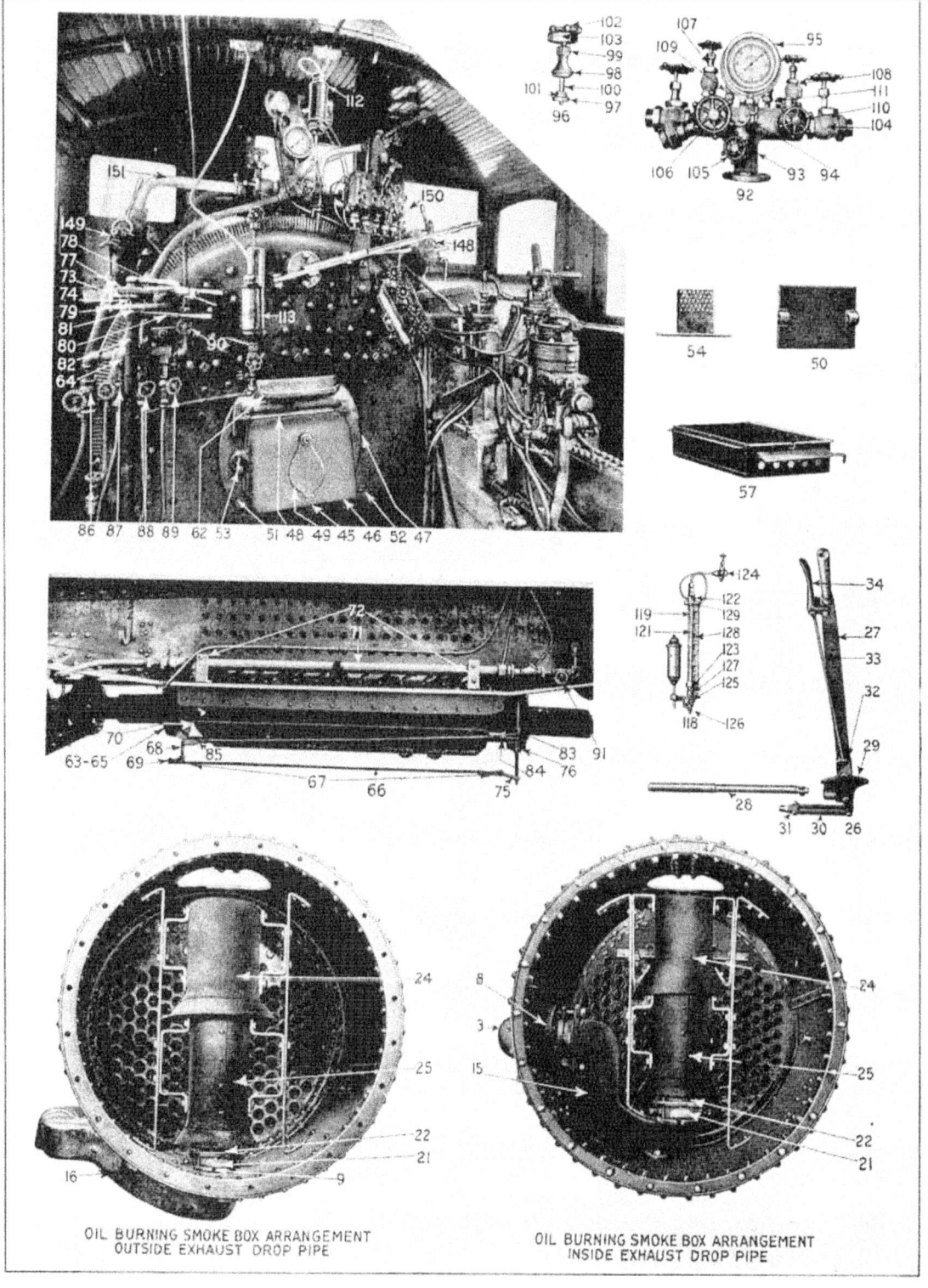

OIL BURNING SMOKE BOX ARRANGEMENT
OUTSIDE EXHAUST DROP PIPE

OIL BURNING SMOKE BOX ARRANGEMENT
INSIDE EXHAUST DROP PIPE

PLATES 7 and 8

Inside Cab Fittings, Smoke Box Arrangement, Ash Pan and Details

CODE WORD	FIG.	NAME OF PART
Rabble	1	Exhaust pipe elbow, coal burning locomotive
Rabid	2	Exhaust pipe elbow, wood burning locomotive
Race	3	Exhaust pipe elbow, oil burning locomotive
Radiant	4	Exhaust pipe flange, coal burning locomotive
Radical	5	Exhaust pipe flange, coal burning locomotive
Rage	6	Exhaust pipe flange, wood burning locomotive
Raging	7	Exhaust pipe flange, wood burning locomotive
Rail	8	Exhaust pipe flange, oil burning locomotive
Raillery	9	Exhaust pipe flange, oil burning locomotive
Raiment	10	Exhaust drop pipe, coal burning locomotive
Raise	11	Exhaust drop pipe, coal burning locomotive
Rake	12	Exhaust drop pipe, coal burning locomotive
Rakish	13	Exhaust drop pipe, wood burning locomotive
Rally	14	Exhaust drop pipe, wood burning locomotive
Ramble	15	Exhaust drop pipe, oil burning locomotive
Rampant	16	Exhaust drop pipe, oil burning locomotive
Rancid	17	Exhaust drop pipe joint ring, coal, wood and oil burning locomotive
Rancor	18	Exhaust drop pipe gland, coal, wood and oil burning locomotive
Random	19	Exhaust pipe extension, coal burning locomotive
Range	20	Exhaust pipe extension, coal burning locomotive
Rankle	21	Exhaust nozzle, coal, wood and oil burning locomotive
Ransack	22	Exhaust nozzle tip, coal, wood and oil burning locomotive
Rant	23	Petticoat pipe, coal burning locomotive
Rapid	24	Petticoat pipe top, wood and oil burning locomotive
Rapidity	25	Petticoat pipe bottom, wood and oil burning locomotive
Rapture	26	THROTTLE LEVER COMPLETE
Rare	27	Throttle lever
Rarefy	28	Throttle lever stem, stub end
Rascal	29	Throttle lever quadrant
Rather	30	Throttle lever link
Ratify	31	Throttle lever fulcrum
Rational	32	Throttle lever latch
Ravage	33	Throttle lever latch lifter
Ravel	34	Throttle lever latch handle
Raving	35	THROTTLE STEM STUFFING BOX COMPLETE
Raze	36	Throttle stem stuffing box
Reach	37	Throttle stem stuffing box gland
React	38	FIREDOOR COMPLETE, WOOD AND COAL BURNING LOCOMOTIVES
Real	39	Firedoor
Really	40	Firedoor liner
Realm	41	Firedoor ring
Reason	42	Firedoor latch
Reassure	43	Firedoor latch guide
Rebel	44	Firedoor pin
Rebound	45	FIREDOOR COMPLETE, OIL BURNING LOCOMOTIVE
Rebuff	46	Firedoor
Rebuke	47	Firedoor ring
Recall	48	Firedoor hinge pin
Recant	49	Firedoor peep hole cover
Recede	50	Firedoor damper
Receipt	51	Firedoor damper, thumb nut stud
Recent	52	Firedoor damper, thumb nuts
Recess	53	Firedoor latch stud
Recital	54	Firedoor deflector plate
Reckless	55	ASH PAN COMPLETE, COAL AND WOOD BURNING LOCOMOTIVES (See Note Page 24)
Reckon	56	Ash pan, coal and wood burning locomotive (See Note Page 24)
Reclaim	57	Oil pan, oil burning locomotive
Recline	58	Grate shaker shaft, coal burning locomotive
Recluse	59	Grate shaker shaft handle, coal burning locomotive
Recoil	60	Grate shaker shaft bracket, top, coal burning locomotive
Recollect	61	Grate shaker shaft bracket, bottom, coal burning locomotive
Reconcile	62	Oil can shelf, coal, wood and oil burning locomotive

PLATES 7 and 8—(Continued)

CODE WORD	FIG.	NAME OF PART	CODE WORD	FIG.	NAME OF PART
Recondite	63	Oil burner (no illustration) oil burning locomotives	Region	100	Master valve stem
Record	64	Oil burner turret, oil burning locomotive	Register	101	Master valve stem nut
			Regret	102	Hand wheel
Recount	65	Oil cock at burner (no illustration) oil burning locomotive	Regular	103	Bonnet ring
			Rehearse	104	Injector valve
			Reign	105	Blower angle valve
			Reinvest	106	Syphon angle valve
Recourse	66	Oil cock rod, oil burning locomotives	Reiterate	107	Air brake angle valve
			Reject	108	Steam brake angle valve
Recover	67	Oil cock rod jaw, oil burning locomotives	Rejoice	109	Steam gauge valve
			Rejoinder	110	Lubricator angle valve
Recreant	68	Oil cock shaft, oil burning locomotives	Rekindle	111	Brake lubricator angle valve
			Relapse	112	Cab lamp
Recruit	69	Oil cock shaft arm, oil burning locomotive	Relate	113	Steam gauge
			Relation	114	Air gauge, equalizing and main reservoir, 5½ in.
Rectify	70	Oil cock shaft hanger, oil burning locomotive			
			Relax	115	Air gauge brake cylinder and brake pipe, 3½ in.
Rectitude	71	OIL HEATER COMPLETE, OIL BURNING LOCOMOTIVE			
			Release	116	Gauge cock
			Relegate	117	Gauge cock dripper
Recumbent	72	Oil heater supports	Relent	118	WATER GLASS COMPLETE, TUBULAR TYPE, COAL, WOOD AND OIL BURNING LOCOMOTIVES
Recur	73	Oil regulator bracket			
Recurrent	74	Oil regulator shaft			
Recusant	75	Oil regulator shaft arm			
Redeem	76	Oil regulator shaft hanger			
Redolence	77	Oil regulator quadrant	Relevant	119	Glass
Redolent	78	OIL REGULATOR LEVER COMPLETE, OIL BURNING LOCOMOTIVE	Reliance	120	Glass gasket, (no illustration)
			Relict	121	Glass shield
			Relieve	122	Top connection
Redouble	79	Oil damper regulator quadrant	Relish	123	Bottom connection
			Reluctant	124	Top valve
Redound	80	Oil damper regulator handle	Rely	125	Bottom valve
Redress	81	Oil damper regulator shaft	Remain	126	Drain valve
Reduce	82	Oil damper regulator shaft bushing	Remark	127	Lamp and marker bracket
			Remedial	128	Marker
Reduction	83	Oil damper regulator arm	Remedy	129	Marker bracket
Re-echo	84	Oil damper rod jaw, front	Remiss	130	WATER GLASS COMPLETE, REFLEX KLINGER TYPE, COAL, WOOD AND OIL BURNING LOCOMOTIVES
Refer	85	Oil damper rod jaw, back			
Referable	86	Oil blower valve			
Referee	87	Oil burner valve			
Refined	88	Oil blow-back valve			
Refit	89	Oil heater valve	Remittent	131	Body, front
Reflect	90	Oil tank heater valve	Remorse	132	Body, back
Reflux	91	Oil pipe valve	Remote	133	Glass
Reform	92	STEAM TURRET COMPLETE, COAL, WOOD AND OIL BURNING LOCOMOTIVES	Rend	134	Glass gaskets, (no illustration)
			Render	135	Top connection or stem
			Renegade	136	Bottom connection or stem
			Renew	137	Bolts, long and short, (no illustration)
Refrain	93	Steam turret			
Refresh	94	Lamp bracket			
Refuge	95	Steam gauge bracket	Renitent	138	Copper washer, (no illustration)
Refute	96	MASTER VALVE COMPLETE, COAL, WOOD AND OIL BURNING LOCOMOTIVES			
			Renounce	139	Top valve
			Renovate	140	Bottom valve
			Renown	141	Lubricator
Regain	97	Master valve	Rent	142	Lubricator steam pipe
Regale	98	Stuffing box	Reparable	143	Lubricator oil pipe, rear cylinder
Reparable	99	Stuffing box nut			

PLATES 7 and 8—(Continued)

CODE WORD	FIG.	NAME OF PART	CODE WORD	FIG.	NAME OF PART
Repay	144	Lubricator oil pipe, middle cylinder	*Represent*	154	Brake valve stuffing box nut
			Repress	155	Brake valve base
Repeal	145	Lubricator oil pipe, front cylinder	*Reprieve*	156	Brake valve cap
			Reprimand	157	Brake valve
Repent	146	Lubricator oil pipe for air brake	*Reprisal*	158	Brake valve stem
			Reproach	159	BRAKE VALVE COMPLETE, COAL, WOOD AND OIL BURNING LOCOMOTIVES
Repine	147	Lubricator oil pipe for steam brake valve			
Replace	148	Injector, right			
Replenish	149	Injector, left	*Reprove*	160	Brake valve handle
Replete	150	Injector steam pipe, right	*Repudiate*	161	Brake valve stuffing box
Replicate	151	Injector steam pipe, left	*Repulsive*	162	Brake valve stuffing box nut
Report	152	BRAKE VALVE COMPLETE, COAL, WOOD AND OIL BURNING LOCOMOTIVES	*Reputable*	163	Brake valve base
			Request	164	Brake valve cap
			Require	165	Brake valve
Repose	153	Brake valve handle	*Requite*	166	Brake valve stem

NOTE.—All orders must specify SHOP NUMBER of locomotive and the "CODE WORD" of the part wanted.

When ordering copper pipes, to insure couplings fitting, we will require the following information:—Pipes for lubricator, give manufacturer's name of lubricator and manufacturer's name and type of valve at turret end of pipe. Pipes for injectors, give manufacturer's name of injector and manufacturer's name and type of valve at turret end of pipe. When ordering lubricators and injector valves, give maker's name and type of valve on locomotive.

When ash pan is ordered complete damper rigging will be included; also state fuel you are using.

In preparing order, read over instructions for ordering carefully to see that you have covered all that is needed to enable us to fill order.

PLATE 9
Stacks, Grates and Details

CODE WORD	FIG.	NAME OF PART	CODE WORD	FIG.	NAME OF PART
Earn	1	Taper stack	*Elder*	15	Rocker grate
Ebriety	2	Taper stack hood	*Elegy*	16	Dump grate
Echo	3	DIAMOND STACK COMPLETE	*Elevate*	17	Side rail, right
			Elicit	18	Side rail, left
Ecstasy	4	Diamond stack ring	*Elision*	19	PLAIN GRATES COMPLETE FOR WOOD BURNING—See Note
Edible	5	Diamond stack cone			
Edifice	6	Diamond stack netting			
Educe	7	Stack saddle, Diamond stack or Radley & Hunter stack	*Elude*	20	Plain grates
Efface	8	RADLEY & HUNTER STACK COMPLETE	*Emanate*	21	Grate support, front
			Embitter	22	Grate support, rear
Effete	9	Radley & Hunter stack ring	*Emerge*	23	Side plates, right
Effigy	10	Radley & Hunter stack cone	*Emulate*	24	Side plates, left
Effuse	11	RADLEY & HUNTER STACK CINDER POT COMPLETE	*Enamor*	25	COVER PLATES COMPLETE FOR WOOD BURNING ON ROCKER GRATES
Egress	12	Radley & Hunter stack cinder pot			
Eject	13	Radley & Hunter stack cinder pot cap	*Engird*	26	Front plate
			Engorge	27	Rear plate
Elated	14	ROCKER GRATES COMPLETE FOR COAL BURNING—See Note	*Engulf*	28	Right plate
			Enhance	29	Left plate

NOTE.—All orders must specify the SHOP NUMBER of locomotive and the "CODE WORD" of the part wanted.

Figure 14 Rocker grates complete includes Figures 15, 16, 17 and 18. When rocker grates only are wanted order Figure 15 and specify number of pieces required.

Figure 19 Plain grates complete includes Figures 20, 21, 22, 23 and 24. When plain grates only are wanted order Figure 20 and specify number of pieces required.

In preparing order, read over instructions for ordering carefully to see that you have covered all that is needed to enable us to fill order.

PLATE 9

Stacks, Grates and Details

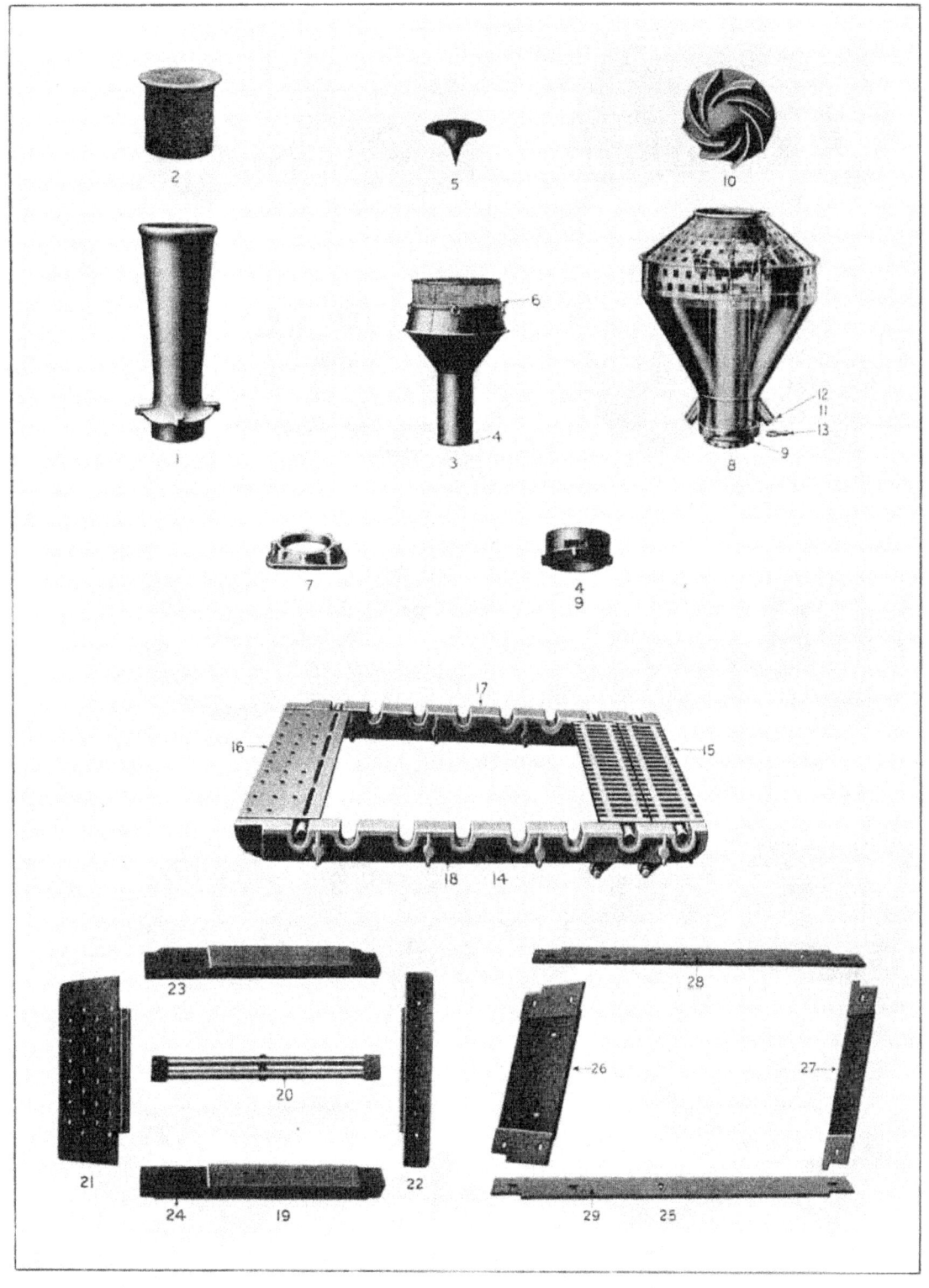

PLATE 10

Trucks and Truck Details

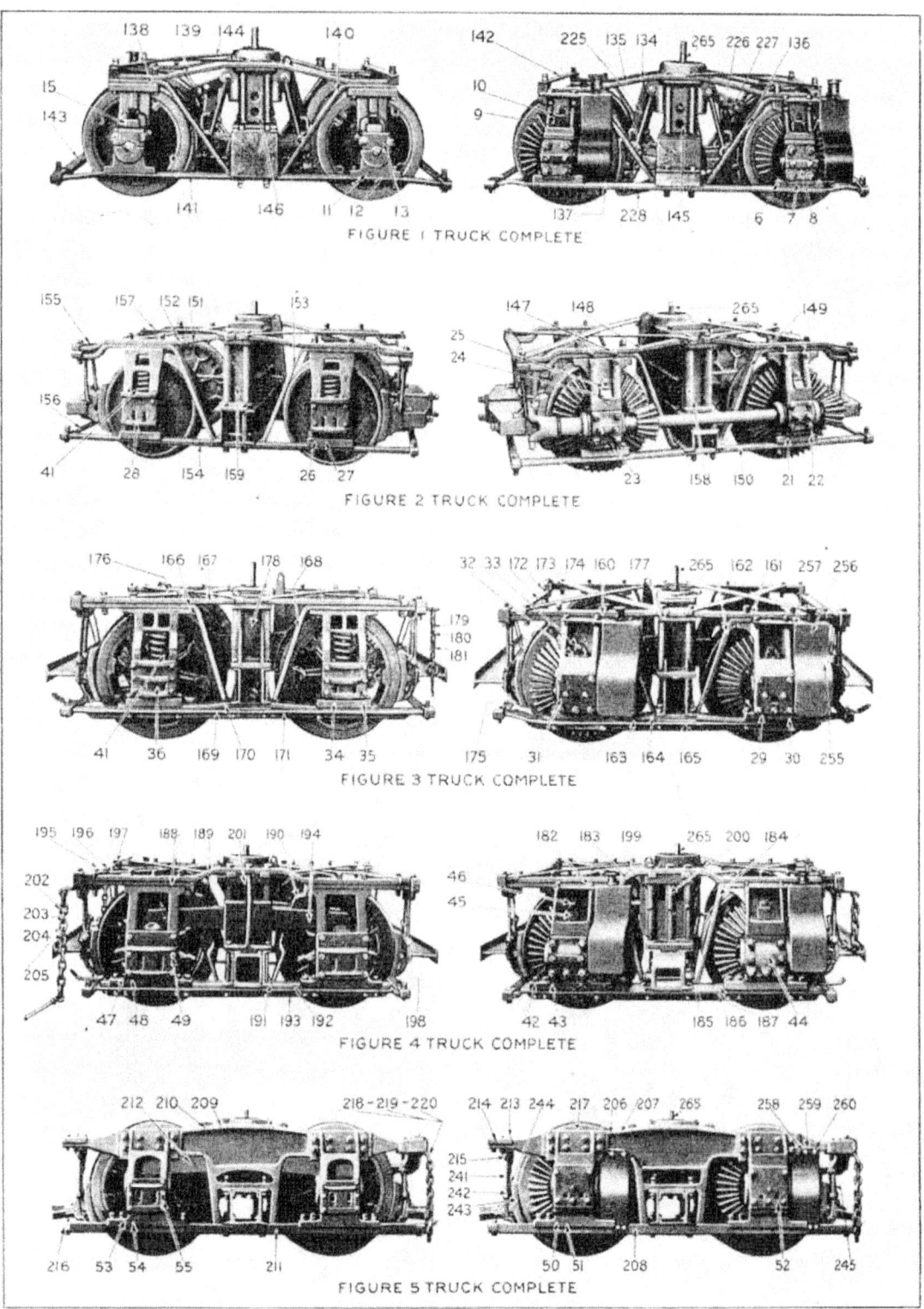

PLATE 11

Trucks and Truck Details

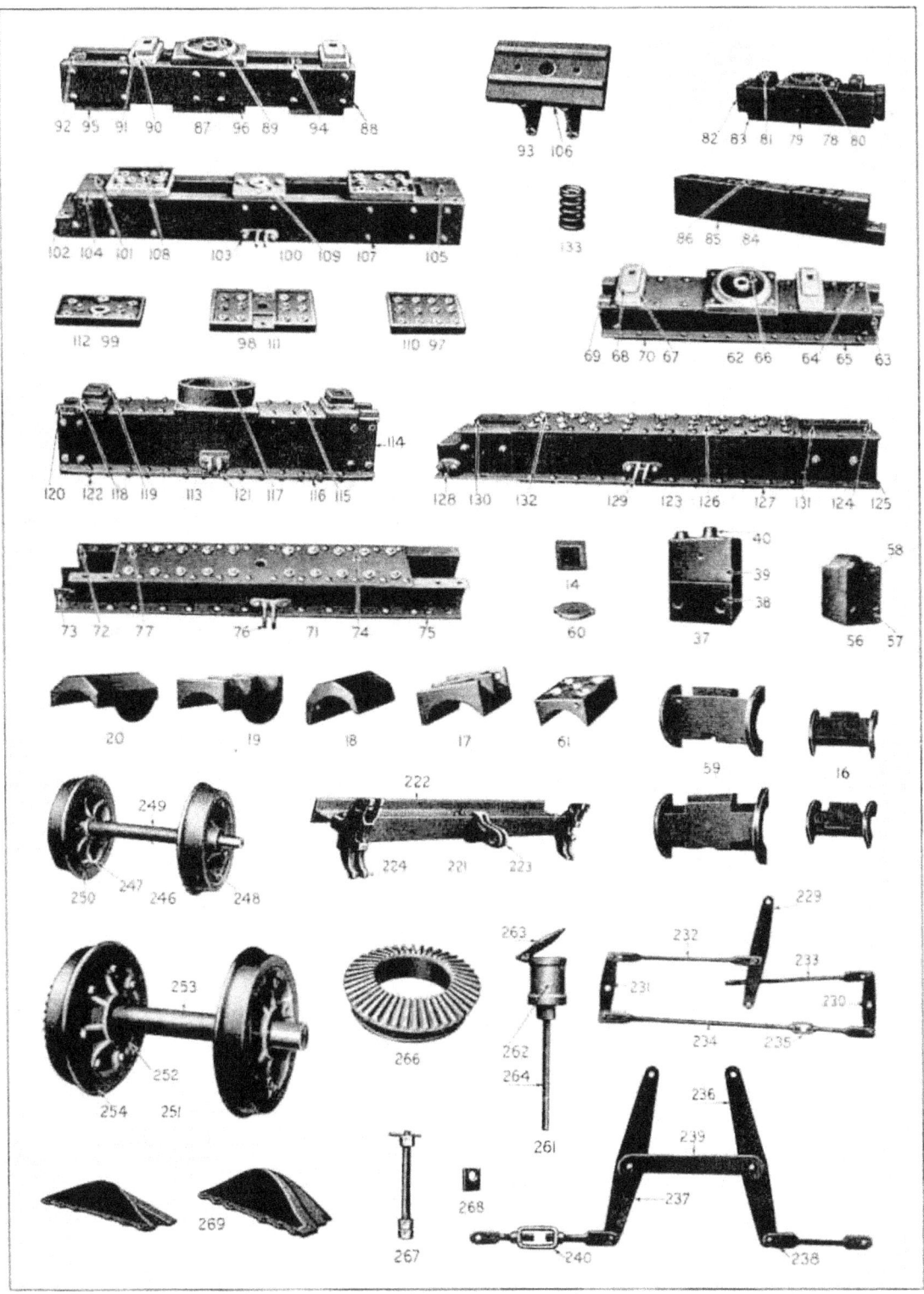

PLATES 10 and 11

Trucks and Truck Details

CODE WORD	FIG.	NAME OF PART
Tabard	1	TRUCK COMPLETE (Used on Class A, two truck locomotives) See Note
Tabaret	2	TRUCK COMPLETE (Used on Class A, two truck locomotives) See Note
Tabasco	3	TRUCK COMPLETE (Used on Class B and C, two and three truck locomotives) See Note
Tabby	4	TRUCK COMPLETE (Used on Class B, C and D, two, three and four truck locomotives) See Note
Tabernacle	5	TRUCK COMPLETE (Cast Steel, used on Class B, C and D locomotives) See Note
Tabes	6	RIGHT TRUCK BOX COMPLETE, front and rear truck, Fig. 1 truck
Tabinet	7	Right truck box naked, front and rear truck
Tablature	8	Right truck box cap, front and rear truck
Table	9	Oil box cover, front and rear truck
Tableau	10	Oil box cover hinge lug, front and rear truck
Tablier	11	LEFT TRUCK PEDESTAL COMPLETE, front and rear truck, Fig. 1 truck
Taboo	12	Left truck pedestal naked, front and rear truck
Taboret	13	Left truck pedestal cap, front and rear truck
Tabular	14	Thrust plate, front and rear truck
Tabulate	15	Oil box cover, front and rear truck
Tache	16	Line shaft brasses, pair, front and rear truck, Fig. 1 truck. See Note
Tacit	17	Journal brass, front and rear truck, Fig. 1 truck. See Note
Tack	18	Journal brass, front and rear truck, Fig. 1 truck. See Note
Taglia	19	Journal brass, front and rear truck, Fig. 1 truck. See Note
Tahr	20	Journal brass, front and rear truck, Fig. 1 truck. See Note

CODE WORD	FIG.	NAME OF PART
		NOTE.—Journal brasses for old style truck boxes are shown on Plate 11, under Fig. 18. Journal brasses with Thrust Plate cast integral for old style truck pedestals are shown on Plate 11, under Figs. 19-20.
Tailage	21	RIGHT TRUCK BOX COMPLETE, front and rear truck, Fig. 2 truck
Tailor	22	Right truck box naked, front and rear truck
Talapoin	23	Right truck box cap, front and rear truck
Talaria	24	Oil box cover, front and rear truck
Talbot	25	Oil box cover hinge lug, front and rear truck
Talc	26	LEFT TRUCK PEDESTAL COMPLETE, front and rear truck, Fig. 2 truck
Talent	27	Left truck pedestal naked, front and rear truck
Talesman	28	Left truck pedestal cap, front and rear truck
Talipes	29	RIGHT TRUCK BOX COMPLETE, front, second and rear truck, Fig. 3 truck
Tallage	30	Right truck box naked, front, second and rear truck
Tallow	31	Right truck box cap, front, second and rear truck
Talmud	32	Oil box cover, front, second and rear truck
Talon	33	Oil box cover hinge lug, front, second and rear truck
Talus	34	LEFT TRUCK PEDESTAL COMPLETE, front, second and rear truck, Fig. 3 truck
Tamale	35	Left truck, pedestal naked, front, second and rear truck
Tambac	36	Left truck pedestal cap, front, second and rear truck
Tambour	37	INSIDE BOX COMPLETE, left truck pedestal, front, second and rear truck, Fig. 3 truck
Tame	38	Inside box naked, left truck pedestal, front, second and rear truck
Taminy	39	Inside box cap, front, second and rear truck
Tamper	40	Inside box spring center, front, second and rear truck
Tandem	41	Inside box spring, front, second and rear truck

PLATES 10 and 11—(Continued)

CODE WORD	FIG.	NAME OF PART
Tang	42	RIGHT TRUCK BOX COMPLETE, front, second, third and rear truck, Fig. 4 truck
Tangent	43	Right truck box naked, front, second, third and rear truck
Tangle	44	Right truck box cap, front, second, third and rear truck
Tango	45	Oil box cover, front, second, third and rear truck
Tangram	46	Oil box cover, hinge lug, front, second, third and rear truck
Tankard	47	LEFT TRUCK PEDESTAL COMPLETE, front, second, third and rear truck, Fig. 4 truck
Tanner	48	Left truck pedestal naked, front, second, third and rear truck
Tannic	49	Left truck pedestal cap, front, second, third and rear truck
Tansy	50	RIGHT TRUCK BOX COMPLETE, front, second and rear truck, Fig. 5 truck
Tantrum	51	Right truck box naked, front, second and rear truck
Tape	52	Right truck box cap, front, second and rear truck
Tapestry	53	LEFT TRUCK PEDESTAL COMPLETE, front, second and rear truck, Fig. 5 truck
Tapioca	54	Left truck pedestal naked, front, second and rear truck
Tapir	55	Left truck pedestal cap, front, second and rear truck
Tapster	56	INSIDE BOX COMPLETE, left truck pedestal, front, second, third and rear truck, Fig. 4 and 5 truck
Tarsal	57	Inside box naked, left truck pedestal, front, second, third and rear truck
Tarsus	58	Inside box cap, left truck pedestal, front, second, third and rear truck
Tartan	59	Line shaft brasses, pair, front, second, third and rear truck, Fig. 2, 3, 4, 5 truck
Task	60	Thrust plate left truck pedestal, front, second, third and rear truck, Fig. 2, 3, 4, 5 truck
Tassel	61	Journal brasses, front, second, third and rear truck, Fig. 2, 3, 4, 5 truck
Taste	62	TOP BOLSTER COMPLETE (Used on Fig. 1, 2, 3 trucks)
Tatter	63	Top bolster channels
Tattoo	64	Top bolster top plate
Taube	65	Top bolster bottom plate
Taunt	66	Top bolster center plate
Tautog	67	Top bolster side bearing base
Tavern	68	Top bolster side bearing block
Tawdry	69	Top bolster end casting
Tazza	70	Top bolster spring center
Teach	71	BOTTOM BOLSTER COMPLETE (Used on Fig. 1, 2, 3 trucks)
Teak	72	Bottom bolster front channel
Technic	73	Bottom bolster rear channel
Tedious	74	Bottom bolster top plate
Teeth	75	Bottom bolster bottom plate
Teledu	76	Bottom bolster brake lever fulcrum
Telekino	77	Bottom bolster spring center
Telescope	78	TOP BOLSTER COMPLETE, wood bolster (Used on Fig. 1 trucks) (Not recommended, shown for details only)
Telesis	79	Top bolster, wood bolster bare
Telic	80	Top bolster center plate
Telltale	81	Top bolster side bearing block
Telluric	82	Top bolster end casting
Temerity	83	Top bolster spring plate
Temperate	84	BOTTOM BOLSTER COMPLETE wood bolster (Used on Fig. 1 truck) (Not recommended, shown for details only)
Tempest	85	Bottom wood bolster bare
Templar	86	Bottom bolster spring plate
Tempter	87	TOP BOLSTER COMPLETE (Not recommended, shown for details only)
Tenable	88	Top bolster channels
Tenace	89	Top bolster center plate
Tenant	90	Top bolster side bearing base
Tend	91	Top bolster side bearing block
Tendon	92	Top bolster end casting
Tendril	93	Top bolster center plate separator
Tenet	94	Top bolster plain separator
Tenon	95	Top bolster spring plate, end
Tense	96	Top bolster spring plate, center
Tensile	97	Top bolster spring plate, end
Tent	98	Top bolster spring plate, center

PLATES 10 and 11—(Continued)

CODE WORD	FIG.	NAME OF PART	CODE WORD	FIG.	NAME OF PART
Tenuity	99	Top bolster spring plate, center	Thwart	132	Bottom bolster spring center
		Note:—Other styles sometimes used for 95 and 96	Thyme	133	Bolster spring (Used on all styles trucks)
Tenure	100	BOTTOM BOLSTER COMPLETE (Not recommended, shown for details only)	Tiara	134	RIGHT TRUCK FRAME COMPLETE, Fig. 1 truck
			Tibia	135	Top arch bar
			Tidal	136	Inverted arch bar
Tepid	101	Bottom bolster channel, front	Tidy	137	Bottom arch or tie bar
Teraph	102	Bottom bolster channel, rear	Tiger	138	LEFT TRUCK FRAME COMPLETE, Fig. 1 truck
Terce	103	Bottom bolster brake lever fulcrum	Tilde	139	Top arch bar
Termite	104	Bottom bolster end casting right	Tiller	140	Inverted arch bar
			Timid	141	Bottom arch or tie bar
Terra	105	Bottom bolster end casting left	Timothy	142	Top crosstie bar
			Tincal	143	Bottom crosstie bar
Terrapin	106	Bottom bolster center separator	Tincture	144	Diagonal brace bar
			Tingle	145	Truck column, right
Terret	107	Bottom bolster plain separator	Tinto	146	Truck column, left
			Tippet	147	RIGHT TRUCK FRAME COMPLETE, Fig. 2 truck
Testudo	108	Bottom bolster spring plate end	Tirade	148	Top arch bar
Tetanus	109	Bottom bolster spring plate, center	Tirwit	149	Inverted arch bar
			Tissue	150	Bottom arch or tie bar
Tether	110	Bottom bolster spring plate, end	Titanic	151	LEFT TRUCK FRAME COMPLETE, Fig. 2 truck
Tetra	111	Bottom bolster spring plate, center	Tithe	152	Top arch bar
			Titrate	153	Inverted arch bar
Texture	112	Bottom bolster spring plate, center	Titular	154	Bottom arch or tie bar
			Toad	155	Top crosstie bar
		Note:—Other styles sometimes used for 108 and 109	Toast	156	Bottom crosstie bar
			Tobine	157	Diagonal brace bar
Thaw	113	TOP BOLSTER COMPLETE (Used on Fig. 4 and 5 trucks)	Toby	158	Truck column, right
			Tocsin	159	Truck column, left
			Toga	160	RIGHT TRUCK FRAME COMPLETE, Fig. 3 truck
Theban	114	Top bolster channels			
Theca	115	Top bolster top plate	Toggle	161	Top arch bar
Theocrat	116	Top bolster bottom plate	Tokay	162	Inverted arch bar
Therm	117	Top bolster center plate	Toledo	163	Bottom arch or tie bar complete, Fig. 3 truck
Thesis	118	Top bolster side bearing base			
Thicket	119	Top bolster side bearing block	Tolerate	164	Bar
Thistle	120	Top bolster end casting	Toman	165	Angle
Thong	121	Top bolster brake stop lug	Tombac	166	LEFT TRUCK FRAME COMPLETE, Fig. 3 truck
Thorax	122	Top bolster spring center			
Thrall	123	BOTTOM BOLSTER COMPLETE (Used on Fig. 4, 5 trucks)	Tomin	167	Top arch bar
			Tompion	168	Inverted arch bar
			Tongs	169	Bottom arch or tie bar complete, Fig. 3 truck
Thread	124	Bottom bolster channels front			
Thresch	125	Bottom bolster channels rear	Tonic	170	Bar
Throb	126	Bottom bolster top plate	Tonite	171	Angle
Thrush	127	Bottom bolster bottom plate	Tonka	172	TOP CROSSTIE BAR COMPLETE, Fig. 3 truck
Thud	128	Bottom bolster bolt washer			
Thule	129	Bottom bolster brake lever fulcrum	Tontine	173	Bar
			Topaz	174	Brake hanger lug
Thunder	130	Bottom bolster end casting right (Not used on Fig. 5 truck)	Tophet	175	Bottom crosstie bar
			Topmast	176	Diagonal brace bars, See Note
			Topsail	177	Truck column, right
Thwack	131	Bottom bolster end casting left (Not used on Fig. 5 truck)	Toque	178	Truck column, left
			Torah	179	Truck safety chain, front truck

PLATES 10 and 11—(Continued)

CODE WORD	FIG.	NAME OF PART	CODE WORD	FIG.	NAME OF PART
Torch	180	Truck safety chain, center truck	*Tressle*	221	BRAKE BEAM COMPLETE, ALL STYLE TRUCKS
Tonada	181	Truck safety chain, rear truck			
Torose	182	RIGHT TRUCK FRAME COMPLETE, Fig. 4 truck	*Triable*	222	Brake beam
			Triad	223	Brake beam lever fulcrum
Torpid	183	Top arch bar	*Triangle*	224	Brake head
Torpor	184	Inverted arch bar	*Tribal*	225	Brake lever long, Fig. 1 truck
Torque	185	BOTTOM ARCH OR TIE BAR COMPLETE, Fig. 4 truck	*Tribasic*	226	Brake lever short, Fig. 1 truck
			Tribe	227	Brake lever stop rod, Fig. 1 truck
Torsion	186	Bar	*Tribrach*	228	Brake rod bottom, Fig. 1 truck
Torso	187	Angle	*Tribunal*	229	Bolster brake lever—Used on Fig. 2, 3, 4 trucks
Tortile	188	LEFT TRUCK FRAME COMPLETE, Fig. 4 truck			
			Tribune	230	Beam brake lever—straight—Used on style Fig. 2, 3, 4 trucks
Torus	189	Top arch bar			
Tory	190	Inverted arch bar			
Totem	191	BOTTOM ARCH OR TIE BAR COMPLETE, Fig. 4 truck	*Tribute*	231	Beam brake lever—offset—Used on Fig. 2, 3, 4 trucks
			Trice	232	Brake rod, top—Used on Fig. 2, 3, 4 trucks
Toucan	192	Bar			
Tout	193	Angle	*Triceps*	233	Brake stop rod—Used on Fig. 2, 3, 4 trucks
Towage	194	Equalizer			
Toxin	195	TOP CROSSTIE BAR COMPLETE, Fig. 4 truck	*Trichord*	234	Brake rod, bottom—Used on Fig. 2, 3, 4 trucks
Tractate	196	Bar	*Trickle*	235	Brake rod turn buckle—Used on Fig. 2, 3, 4 trucks
Tractrix	197	Brake hanger lug			
Traduce	198	Bottom crosstie bar	*Triclinic*	236	Bolster brake lever—Used on Fig. 5 trucks
Trail	199	Diagonal brace bars—See Note			
			Tricolor	237	Bolster brake lever—Used on Fig. 5 truck
Tramble	200	Truck column, right			
Tramp	201	Truck column, left	*Trifle*	238	Brake rod bottom—Used on Fig. 5 truck
Trance	202	Truck safety chain, front truck			
			Trident	239	Brake lever—Used on Fig. 5 truck
Transept	203	Truck safety chain, second truck			
			Trig	240	Brake rod and turn buckle—Used on Fig. 5 truck
Transfix	204	Truck safety chain, third truck			
			Trigger	241	Brake hanger—all style trucks
Transfuse	205	Truck safety chain, rear truck			
Transom	206	RIGHT TRUCK FRAME COMPLETE, Fig. 5 trucks	*Trigonal*	242	Brake hanger pin—all style trucks
Transude	207	Cast steel frame	*Trilith*	243	Brake shoe—all style trucks
Trapper	208	Bottom arch or tie bar	*Trilogy*	244	Brake shoe key—all style trucks
Travado	209	LEFT TRUCK FRAME COMPLETE, Fig. 5 truck			
			Trinity	245	Brake beam safety chains, Fig. 3, 4, 5 trucks
Travail	210	Cast steel frame			
Trawl	211	Bottom arch or tie bar	*Trio*	246	PAIR CHILLED WHEELS ON AXLE OR PAIR WHEELS WITH TIRES ON AXLE, COMPLETE, Fig. 1, 2 trucks
Treacle	212	Equalizer			
Tread	213	TOP CROSSTIE BAR COMPLETE, Fig. 5 truck			
Treble	214	Bar			
Trefoil	215	Brake hanger lug	*Tripe*	247	Wheel center
Trellis	216	Bottom crosstie bar	*Triple*	248	Chilled wheel
Tremolo	217	Diagonal brace bar—See Note	*Tripod*	249	Axle
Tremor	218	Truck safety chain, front truck	*Tripoli*	250	Tire
			Trisect	251	PAIR WHEELS WITH TIRES, ON AXLE COMPLETE, Fig. 3, 4, 5 trucks
Trepan	219	Truck safety chain, center truck			
Trespass	220	Truck safety chain, rear truck	*Trite*	252	Wheel center

PLATES 10 and 11—(Continued)

CODE WORD	FIG.	NAME OF PART
Triton	253	Axle
Triune	254	Tire
Trivet	255	GEAR COVER COMPLETE, Fig. 1, 2, 3, 4 trucks
Trocha	256	Gear cover
Trojan	257	Gear cover bracket
Troll	258	GEAR COVER COMPLETE, Fig. 5 trucks
Trollop	259	Gear cover
Trope	260	Gear cover tap bolts
Trophy	261	GEAR OIL CUP COMPLETE, all style trucks
Tropical	262	Gear oil cup, all style trucks
Trover	263	Gear oil cup cover, all style trucks
Trudge	264	Gear oil cup pipe, all style trucks
Tucum	265	King bolt, all style trucks
Tundra	266	Gear rim, all style trucks
Tunic	267	Gear rim bolt
Tupelo	268	Gear rim key
Turban	269	Wrecking frogs, one pair, all style trucks

NOTE.—All orders must specify the SHOP NUMBER of locomotive and the "CODE WORD" of part wanted.

When ordering line shaft brasses or journal brasses, give diameter of bearing.

When ordering trucks specify number required and location on engine, whether front, second, third or rear. If only one truck required, give diameter of wheels on remaining trucks.

Two pair of wheels mounted on axles do not constitute a truck. When only wheels mounted on axles are required order in accordance with catalogue and do not order "trucks".

When ordering new wheels or tires to run with old wheels under engine be sure to give diameter of wheels or tires under engine.

When ordering truck parts specify if required for Front, Second, Third or Rear Truck.

Due to diagonal brace bars not being interchangeable, when ordering give location of bars wanted.

Truck illustrated Figure 2 shows wooden brake beams, steel brake beams are now used on this truck same as shown by Figure 221.

For illustration of Class A, B, C and D Shay Locomotives, see Page 4 of this catalogue.

In preparing order, read over instructions for ordering carefully to see that you have covered all that is needed to enable us to fill order.

The gear rims for Shay Locomotives are patented. Replace gear rims should therefore be secured from us in order to avoid patent infringement.

PLATE 12
Tank Valve, Syphon and Details

CODE WORD	FIG.	NAME OF PART
Waft	1	TANK VALVE COMPLETE
Wage	2	Tank valve
Wake	3	Tank valve seat
Wane	4	Tank valve body
Wanton	5	Tank valve plate
Ward	6	Tank valve strainer
Wash	7	Tank flange, top
Watch	8	Tank flange, bottom
Weal	9	Tank flange cap
Weapon	10	Tank valve stem
Weave	11	Tank valve stem handle
Weazen	12	Tank valve stem clamp nut
Weep	13	Tank valve stem nut
Welfare	14	SYPHON COMPLETE
Wield	15	Syphon body
Wind	16	Syphon tube
Wisdom	17	SYPHON PIPE COMPLETE
Witch	18	Syphon pipe flange bottom
Wither	19	Syphon pipe flange top
Wizard	20	Syphon pipe
Wonder	21	Syphon gooseneck
Wondrous	22	Syphon hose
Wood	23	Syphon hose nipple
Work	24	Syphon hose strainer
World	25	Syphon flange
Worry	26	Tank man hole ring
Worship	27	Tank man hole cover
Wound	28	Hose connection union nut
Wrangle	29	Hose connection union nut nipple
Wrap	30	Hose connection nipple
Wrath	31	Hose connection bushing
Wreath	32	OIL TANK VALVE CASE COMPLETE, INCLUDING STRAINER
Wrench	33	OIL TANK VALVE STEM COMPLETE
Wrest	34	Oil tank valve stem handle
Wretch	35	Oil tank valve stem, upper end
Wrought	36	Oil tank valve stem connecting nut
Wroth	37	Oil tank valve stem, lower end (valve attached)
Wrong	38	Oil tank valve spring

NOTE.—All orders must specify SHOP NUMBER of locomotive and the "CODE WORD" of the part wanted.

In preparing order, read over instructions for ordering carefully to see that you have covered all that is needed to enable us to fill order.

PLATE 12

Tank Valve, Syphon and Details

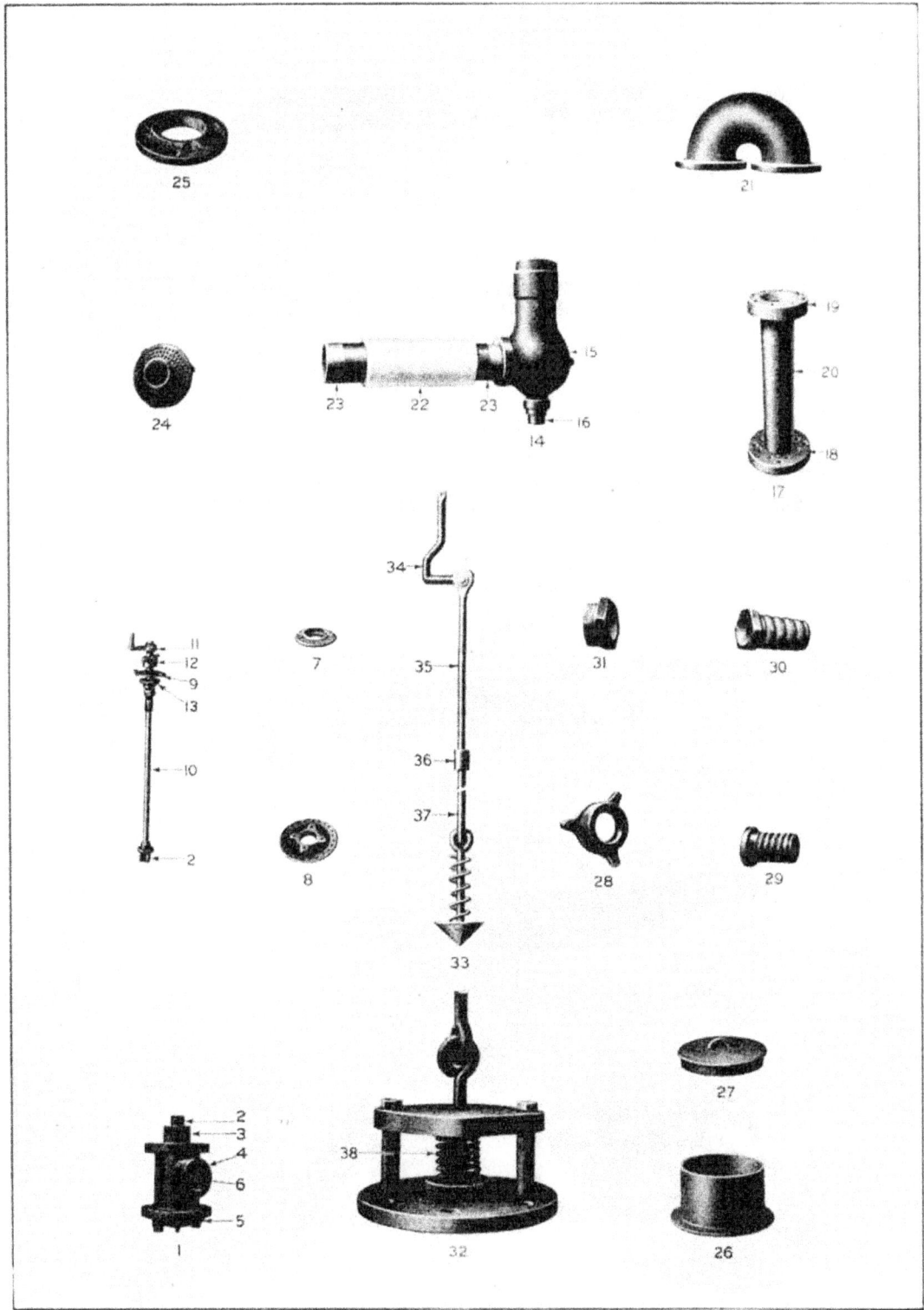

PLATE 13

Engine Frames and Frame Details

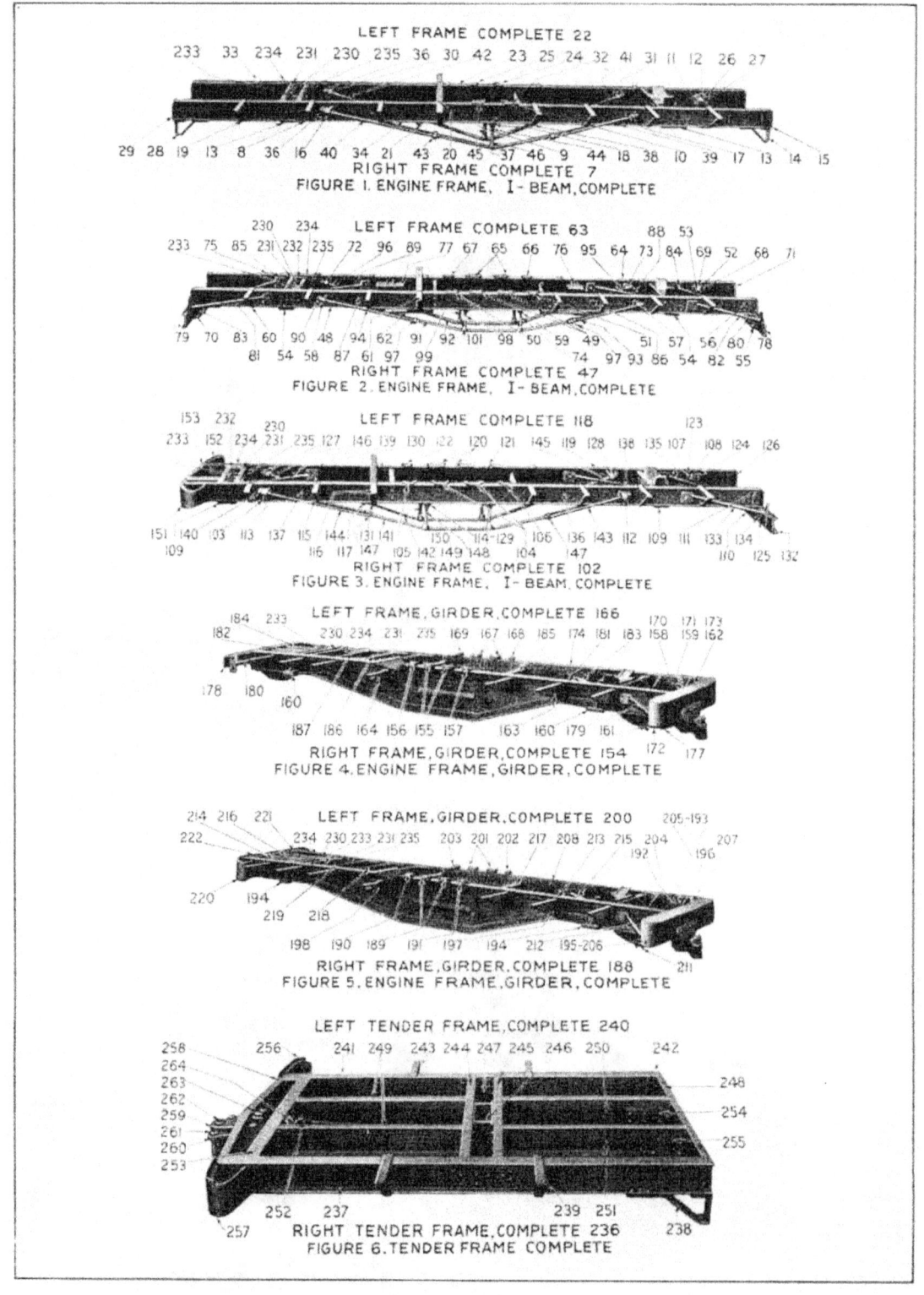

FIGURE 1. ENGINE FRAME, I-BEAM, COMPLETE
FIGURE 2. ENGINE FRAME, I-BEAM, COMPLETE
FIGURE 3. ENGINE FRAME, I-BEAM, COMPLETE
FIGURE 4. ENGINE FRAME, GIRDER, COMPLETE
FIGURE 5. ENGINE FRAME, GIRDER, COMPLETE
FIGURE 6. TENDER FRAME COMPLETE

PLATE 14

Engine Frames and Frame Details

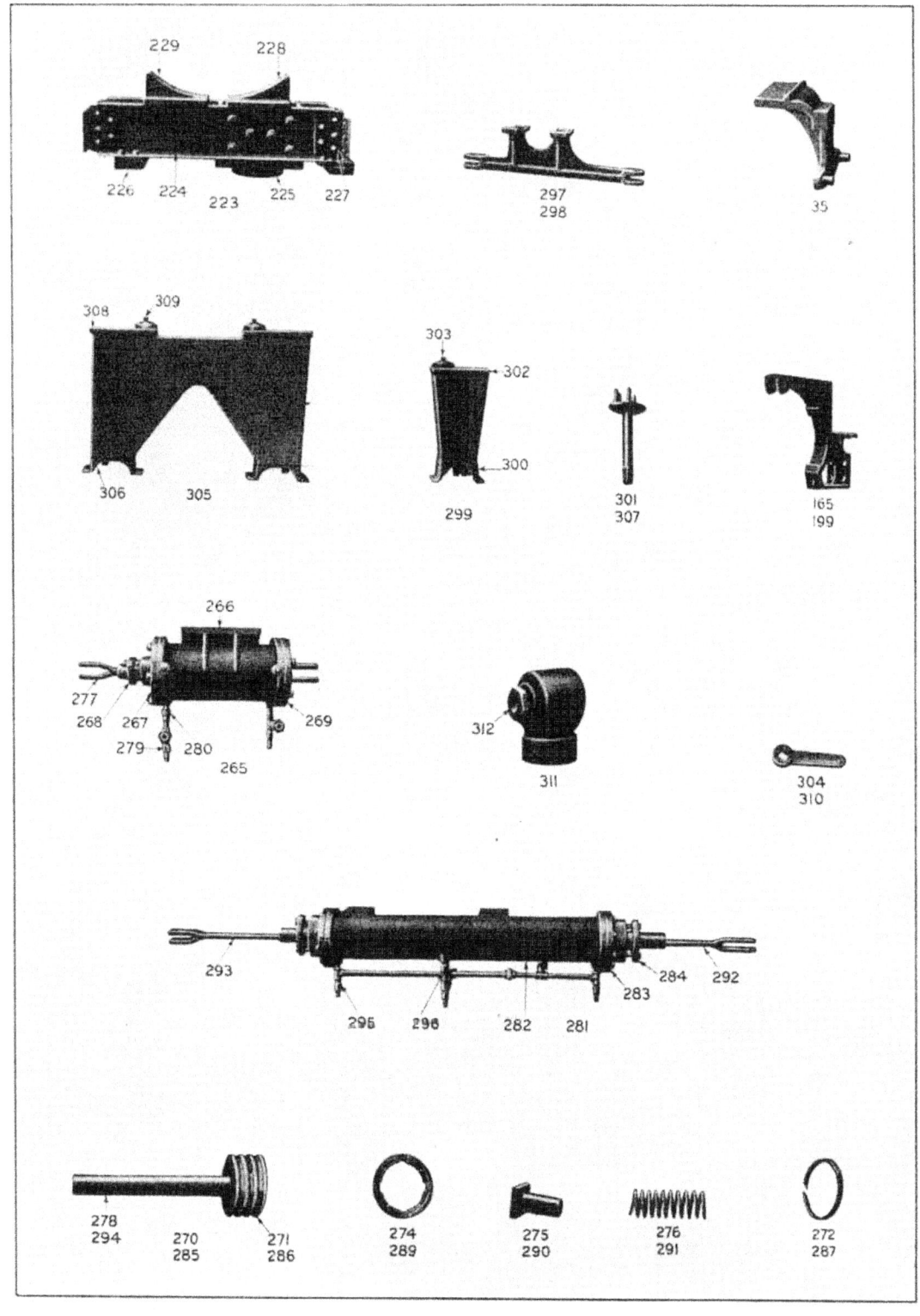

PLATES 13 and 14
Engine Frames and Frame Details

CODE WORD	FIG.	NAME OF PART
Fable	1	RIGHT AND LEFT ENGINE FRAME, I-BEAM, WITH ACCESSORIES TO MAKE FRAME COMPLETE, two truck Class A locomotive
Fabric	2	RIGHT AND LEFT ENGINE FRAME, I-BEAM, WITH ACCESSORIES TO MAKE FRAME COMPLETE, two truck Class B locomotive
Facade	3	RIGHT AND LEFT ENGINE FRAME, I-BEAM, WITH ACCESSORIES TO MAKE FRAME COMPLETE, three and four truck Class C and D locomotives
Faced	4	RIGHT AND LEFT ENGINE FRAME, GIRDER, WITH ACCESSORIES TO MAKE FRAME COMPLETE, two truck Class B locomotive
Facial	5	RIGHT AND LEFT ENGINE FRAME, GIRDER, WITH ACCESSORIES TO MAKE FRAME COMPLETE, three and four truck Class C and D locomotives
Faction	6	RIGHT AND LEFT TENDER FRAME, WITH ACCESSORIES TO MAKE FRAME COMPLETE, used with Fig. 3, 5 frames
Factious	7	RIGHT FRAME, I-BEAM, COMPLETE, Fig. 1 frame
Factor	8	Right frame bare and punched
Faculty	9	Boiler pad clamp, rear
Faddist	10	Boiler pad clamp, front
Fading	11	Frame pad for smoke box brace
Fagot	12	Frame pad pin
Fain	13	Side bearing, right side
Fairy	14	End timber angle brace
Faith	15	Frame angles
Fake	16	Truss pad, right
Falcate	17	Truss pad, left
Falcon	18	Truss post socket
Fallacy	19	Running board brackets
Fallen	20	Reverse lever or quadrant bracket
Fallible	21	Brake lever fulcrum
Fallow	22	LEFT FRAME, I-BEAM, COMPLETE, Fig. 1 frame
False	23	Left frame bare and punched
Falsify	24	Boiler pad clamp, front
Falter	25	Boiler pad clamp, rear
Famed	26	Frame pad for smoke box brace
Famine	27	Frame pad pin
Famish	28	End timber angle brace
Famous	29	Frame angles
Fanatic	30	Truss pad, right
Fancied	31	Truss pad, left
Fancy	32	Truss post socket
Fandango	33	Running board brackets
Fanion	34	Brake lever guides
Fantail	35	Grate shaker shaft bracket
Fantan	36	Truss pad washer
Fantasy	37	Truss rod right side
Farad	38	Truss rod left side
Farce	39	Truss rod end right side, front
Farina	40	Truss rod end right side, rear
Farmer	41	Truss rod end left side, front
Faro	42	Truss rod end left side, rear
Farness	43	Truss heads
Farrier	44	Truss post, right side
Farrow	45	Truss post, left side
Farther	46	Truss post head
Fascia	47	RIGHT FRAME, I-BEAM, COMPLETE, Fig. 2 frame
Fascine	48	Right frame, bare and punched
Fashion	49	Boiler pad clamp, center
Fasten	50	Boiler pad clamp end, rear
Fasting	51	Boiler pad clamp end, front
Fatal	52	Frame pad for smoke box brace
Fate	53	Frame pad bolt and washer
Fathom	54	Side bearing right side
Fatigue	55	End timber angle brace
Falling	56	Frame angles
Fatten	57	Truss pad, right
Fatuity	58	Truss pad, left
Fauces	59	Truss pad socket
Faugh	60	Running board brackets
Faun	61	Reverse lever or quadrant bracket
Favor	62	Brake lever guides
Fawn	63	LEFT FRAME, I-BEAM, COMPLETE, Fig. 2 frame
Faze	64	Left frame bare and punched

PLATES 13 and 14—(Continued)

CODE WORD	FIG.	NAME OF PART
Fealty	65	Boiler pad clamp, center
Feast	66	Boiler pad clamp end—front
Feather	67	Boiler pad clamp end—rear
Feature	68	Frame pad for smoke box brace
Febrile	69	Frame pad bolt and washer
Fecal	70	End timber angle brace
Fecula	71	Frame angles
Feound	72	Truss pad, right
Feeble	73	Truss pad, left
Feign	74	Truss post socket
Feint	75	Running board brackets
Feline	76	Brake cylinder bracket, front
Fellow	77	Brake cylinder bracket, rear
Felon	78	Frame end channel, front
Felspar	79	Frame end channel, rear
Felting	80	Frame brace to end timber right side, outside frame, front
Fence	81	Frame brace to end timber right side, outside frame, rear
Fencing	82	Frame brace to end timber right side between frame, front—See Note
Fender	83	Frame brace to end timber right side between frame, rear—See Note
Fennel	84	Frame brace to end timber left side, between frame, front—See Note
Ferial	85	Frame brace to end timber left side, between frame, rear—See Note

NOTE.—Some locomotives use these braces from bolster to end timber instead of from frame to end timber.

CODE WORD	FIG.	NAME OF PART
Ferment	86	Frame brace to bolster right side, front Figure 2 frame
Fernery	87	Frame brace to bolster right side, rear
Ferocity	88	Frame brace to bolster left side, front
Ferrate	89	Frame brace to bolster left side, rear
Ferretto	90	Truss pad washer
Ferric	91	Truss rod, right side
Ferrous	92	Truss rod, left side
Ferrule	93	Truss rod end right side, front
Ferry	94	Truss rod end right side, rear
Fertile	95	Truss rod end left side, front
Ferule	96	Truss rod end left side, rear
Fervent	97	Truss heads
Fervid	98	Truss post, right side
Fervor	99	Truss post, left side
Festal	100	Truss post guides—(No illustration)
Festival	101	Truss post heads

CODE WORD	FIG.	NAME OF PART
Festoon	102	RIGHT FRAME, I-BEAM, COMPLETE FIGURE 3 FRAME
Fetch	103	Right frame bare and punched
Feticide	104	Boiler pad clamp, center
Fetish	105	Boiler pad clamp, rear
Fetlock	106	Boiler pad clamp, front
Fetter	107	Frame pad for smoke box brace
Fettle	108	Frame pad bolt and washer
Fetus	109	Side bearing right side
Feud	110	End timber angle brace
Fever	111	Frame angles
Fewness	112	Truss pad, right
Fiance	113	Truss pad, left
Fibber	114	Truss post socket
Fibril	115	Running board brackets
Fibroid	116	Reverse lever or quadrant bracket
Fibrous	117	Brake lever fulcrum
Fibula	118	LEFT FRAME, I-BEAM, COMPLETE FIGURE 3 FRAME
Fickle	119	Left frame bare and punched
Fiction	120	Boiler pad clamp, center
Fidalgo	121	Boiler pad clamp, front
Fiddle	122	Boiler pad clamp, rear
Fidelity	123	Frame pad for smoke box brace
Fidget	124	Frame pad bolt and washer
Field	125	End timber angle brace
Fiend	126	Frame angles
Fiery	127	Truss pad, right
Figment	128	Truss pad, left
Figwort	129	Truss post socket
Filar	130	Running board brackets
Filator	131	Brake lever guides
Filbert	132	Frame end channel, front for engine frame
Filch	133	Frame brace to end timber right side outside frame, front
Filiform	134	Frame brace to end timber right side between frame, front
Fling	135	Frame brace to end timber left side between frame, front
Filler	136	Frame brace to bolster right side, front
Fillip	137	Frame brace to bolster right side, rear
Fillister	138	Frame brace to bolster left side, front
Film	139	Frame brace to bolster left side, rear
Filose	140	Truss pad washer
Filter	141	Truss rod, right side

PLATES 13 and 14—(Continued)

CODE WORD	FIG.	NAME OF PART	CODE WORD	FIG.	NAME OF PART
Filtrate	142	Truss rod, left side	*Flaccid*	181	Frame brace to bolster right side, front
Finable	143	Truss rod end right side, front			
Finale	144	Truss rod end right side, rear	*Flageolet*	182	Frame brace to bolster right side, rear
Finality	145	Truss rod end left side, front			
Finance	146	Truss rod end left side, rear	*Flagon*	183	Frame brace to bolster left side front
Finback	147	Truss heads			
Pinch	148	Truss post, right side	*Flake*	184	Frame brace to bolster left side rear
Finder	149	Truss post, left side			
Finely	150	Truss post heads	*Flame*	185	Pit irons
Finesse	151	End casting bracket, right side	*Flang*	186	Frame spreader, front
Finger	152	End casting bracket, left side	*Flanker*	187	Frame spreader, rear
Finial	153	Engine frame end casting	*Flannel*	188	RIGHT FRAME GIRDER COMPLETE, FIGURE 5 FRAME
Finikin	154	RIGHT FRAME GIRDER COMPLETE, FIGURE 4 FRAME			
Finish	155	Boiler pad clamp, center	*Flapper*	189	Boiler pad clamp, center
Finite	156	Boiler pad clamp end, rear	*Flash*	190	Boiler pad clamp, rear
Finlet	157	Boiler pad clamp end, front	*Flashing*	191	Boiler pad clamp, front
Finned	158	Frame pad for smoke box brace	*Flatten*	192	Frame pad for smoke box brace
Finos	159	Frame pad bolt and washer	*Flatting*	193	Frame pad bolt and washer
Finsen	160	Side bearing, right side	*Flatulent*	194	Side bearing, right side
Fiord	161	End timber angle brace	*Flaunt*	195	End timber angle brace
Firearms	162	Frame angles	*Flavor*	196	Frame angles
Firefly	163	Running board brackets	*Flaxen*	197	Running board brackets
Fireside	164	Reverse lever or quadrant bracket	*Fleabane*	198	Reverse lever or quadrant bracket
Firstling	165	Reservoir brackets (This style reservoir bracket also used with Fig. 2 and 3 frame)	*Fleaking*	199	Reservoir brackets
			Flection	200	LEFT FRAME GIRDER COMPLETE, FIGURE 5 FRAME
Firth	166	LEFT FRAME GIRDER COMPLETE, FIGURE 4 FRAME	*Fledge*	201	Boiler pad clamp, center
			Fleece	202	Boiler pad clamp, front
			Flense	203	Boiler pad clamp, rear
Fiscal	167	Boiler pad clamp, center	*Fleshly*	204	Frame pad for smoke box brace
Fisher	168	Boiler pad clamp end, front			
Fishgig	169	Boiler pad clamp end—rear	*Flexor*	205	Frame pad bolt and washer
Fission	170	Frame pad for smoke box brace	*Flexure*	206	End timber angle brace
			Flick	207	Frame angles
Fissure	171	Frame pad bolt and washer	*Flight*	208	Running board brackets
Fistic	172	End timber angle brace, Fig. 4 frame	*Flimsy*	209	Brake cylinder bracket, channel iron, front (No illustration)
Fitness	173	Frame angles			
Fitter	174	Running board brackets	*Flinch*	210	Brake cylinder bracket, channel iron, rear (No illustration)
Fixation	175	Brake cylinder bracket, channel iron, front (No illustration)			
			Flinty	211	Frame end channels front for engine frame
Fixedly	176	Brake cylinder bracket, channel iron, rear (No illustration)	*Flippant*	212	Frame brace to end timber right side outside frame, front
Fixity	177	Frame end channel—front	*Flipper*	213	Frame brace to bolster right side, front
Fixture	178	Frame end channel—rear			
Fizgig	179	Frame brace to end timber right side outside frame—front	*Flirt*	214	Frame brace to bolster right side, rear
			Flirting	215	Frame brace to bolster left side, front
Flabby	180	Frame brace to end timber right side outside frame—rear	*Flitch*	216	Frame brace to bolster left side, rear

PLATES 13 and 14—(Continued)

CODE WORD	FIG.	NAME OF PART	CODE WORD	FIG.	NAME OF PART
Float	217	Pit irons	*Focus*	244	TENDER FRAME BOLSTER COMPLETE, USED WITH FIG. 3 AND 5 ENGINE FRAMES
Floating	218	Frame spreader, front			
Floccose	219	Frame spreader, rear			
Flock	220	End casting bracket, right side			
			Fodder	245	Bolster channels
Flogging	221	End casting bracket, left side	*Foggy*	246	Bolster center plate
Flood	222	Engine frame and casting	*Fohat*	247	Bolster side bearing
Flop	223	ENGINE FRAME BOLSTER, FRONT, COMPLETE USED ON ALL STYLE FRAMES	*Foil*	248	Rear end channel
			Foist	249	Front brace channel
			Fold	250	Rear brace channel, right
			Foliage	251	Rear brace channel, left
Flora	224	Engine frame bolster channels, used on all style frames	*Folio*	252	Shackle bar brace
			Folk	253	Front brace beam
			Folly	254	Drawhead brace, right
Floret	225	Engine frame bolster center plate, used on all style frames	*Foment*	255	Drawhead brace, left
			Fond	256	End casting bracket, right
			Fontal	257	End casting bracket, left
Florist	226	Engine frame bolster side bearing, used on all style frames	*Footing*	258	End casting
			Forage	259	Shackle bar
			Force	260	Safety links
Floss	227	Engine frame bolster angles, used on all style frames	*Forceps*	261	Safety link pins
			Forcible	262	Shackle bar pin
			Forego	263	Shackle bar key
Flotilla	228	Boiler saddle, right	*Ford*	264	Shackle bar gib
Flotsam	229	Boiler saddle, left	*Forest*	265	BRAKE CYLINDER SINGLE PISTON TYPE COMPLETE, ALL STYLE FRAMES
Flounce	230	ENGINE FRAME BOLSTER, REAR, COMPLETE, USED ON ALL STYLE FRAMES			
Flour	231	Engine frame bolster channels, used on all style frames	*Foretop*	266	Brake cylinder barrel
			Forge	267	Brake cylinder head and stuffing box
Flow	232	Engine frame bolster fill block, used on Fig 2, and 3 frames only	*Fork*	268	Brake cylinder head stuffing box gland
			Forlorn	269	Brake cylinder head plain
Fluent	233	Engine frame bolster center plate, used on all style frames	*Fornix*	270	BRAKE CYLINDER PISTON COMPLETE, ALL STYLE FRAMES
			Forte	271	Brake piston head
Fluff	234	Engine frame bolster side bearing, used on all style frames	*Forth*	272	Brake piston head packing spring ring
			Fortify	273	BRAKE PISTON HEAD SECTIONAL PACKING COMPLETE, FOR SINGLE PISTON TYPE CYLINDER, ALL STYLE FRAMES
Fluke	235	Engine frame bolster angles, used on all style frames			
Flush	236	RIGHT TENDER FRAME, COMPLETE, USED WITH FIG. 3 AND 5 ENGINE FRAMES			
			Fortress	274	Sectional ring
Fluster	237	Right frame bare and punched	*Forum*	275	Spring pin
Flute	238	End timber angle brace	*Fossil*	276	Spring
Flutter	239	Running board brackets	*Foster*	277	Piston rod
Flux	240	LEFT TENDER FRAME, COMPLETE, USED WITH FIG. 3 AND 5 ENGINE FRAMES	*Fought*	278	Hollow piston
			Founder	279	Brake cylinder relief valve
			Fount	280	Brake cylinder release check
			Foxy	281	BRAKE CYLINDER DOUBLE PISTON TYPE COMPLETE, ALL STYLE FRAMES — See Note
Flying	241	Left frame bare and punched			
Foal	242	End timber angle brace			
Focal	243	Running board brackets			

PLATES 13 and 14—(Continued)

CODE WORD	FIG.	NAME OF PART	CODE WORD	FIG.	NAME OF PART
Foyer	282	Brake cylinder barrel	*Frigate*	297	Brake cylinder strut, front, all style frames except Fig. 1 frame
Fracas	283	Brake cylinder head and stuffing box	*Fright*	298	Brake cylinder strut, rear, all style frames except Fig. 1 frame
Fragile	284	Brake cylinder head stuffing box gland	*Frigid*	299	SAND BOX SINGLE, COMPLETE
Fragment	285	BRAKE CYLINDER PISTON COMPLETE, ALL STYLE FRAMES—See Note	*Frisk*	300	Sand box base
			Frith	301	Sand box valve
Frail	286	Brake piston head	*Frock*	302	Sand box top
Frank	287	Brake piston head packing spring ring	*Frolic*	303	Sand box lid
			Frond	304	Sand box lever
Frantic	288	BRAKE PISTON HEAD SECTION PACKING COMPLETE, ALL STYLE FRAMES—See Note	*Froth*	305	SAND BOX DOUBLE COMPLETE, ALL STYLE FRAMES EXCEPT FIG. 1 FRAME
Frap	289	Sectional ring	*Frowsy*	306	Sand box base
Fraxin	290	Spring pin	*Frugal*	307	Sand box valve
Frackle	291	Spring	*Fruit*	308	Sand box top
Freeze	292	Brake piston rod, front	*Fudge*	309	Sand box lid
Frenzy	293	Brake piston rod, rear	*Fugal*	310	Sand box lever
Fresco	294	Brake hollow piston	*Fusion*	311	Air sander trap
Fresh	295	Brake cylinder relief valve	*Futile*	312	Air sander trap nozzle
Friar	296	Brake cylinder release check			

NOTE.—All orders must specify the SHOP NUMBER of locomotive and the "CODE WORD" of the part wanted.

When ordering front frame bolster complete, state whether it is wanted with or without boiler saddles.

Some locomotives, 80-ton and over, have double brake cylinders with different size pistons, when ordering details state whether for large or small end.

For illustration of Class A, B, C and D Shay Locomotives, see Page 4 of this catalogue.

In preparing order, read over instructions for ordering carefully to see that you have covered all that is needed to enable us to fill order.

PLATE 15

Draft Gear, Drawheads and Automatic Couplers

CODE WORD	FIG.	NAME OF PART	CODE WORD	FIG.	NAME OF PART
Dabble	1	Drawhead, two pocket used only with Lima Coupler	*Deaf*	13	FRICTION DRAFT GEAR COMPLETE
Daft	2	Drawhead, three pocket link and pin or automatic coupler	*Dearth*	14	Drawhead
			Debar	15	Drawhead pin
			Debase	16	Drawhead guide
Dainty	3	Drawhead, three pocket link and pin for pilot or automatic coupler	*Debauch*	17	Drawhead carrier
			Debility	18	Draft gear connecting rod
			Decadence	19	Draft gear connecting rod pin, upper
Dally	4	Drawhead, three pocket link and pin or automatic coupler	*Decamp*	20	Draft gear connecting rod pin, lower
Dapper	5	Drawhead, three pocket link and pin	*Deciduous*	21	Draft gear connecting rod link
Dastard	6	Drawhead, two pocket link and pin	*Decipher*	22	Draft gear connecting rod link pin
Data	7	Lima automatic coupler complete	*Decisive*	23	Draft gear frame, right side
			Declaim	24	Draft gear frame, left side
Datum	8	Coupler head	*Declivity*	25	Draft gear sliding bar, right side
Daub	9	Coupler knuckle			
Daunt	10	Coupler lock	*Decorum*	26	Draft gear sliding bar, left side
Dawdle	11	Coupler lock shaft			
Dazzle	12	Coupler pin	*Decoy*	27	Draft gear friction plate

PLATE 15

Draft Gear, Drawheads and Automatic Couplers

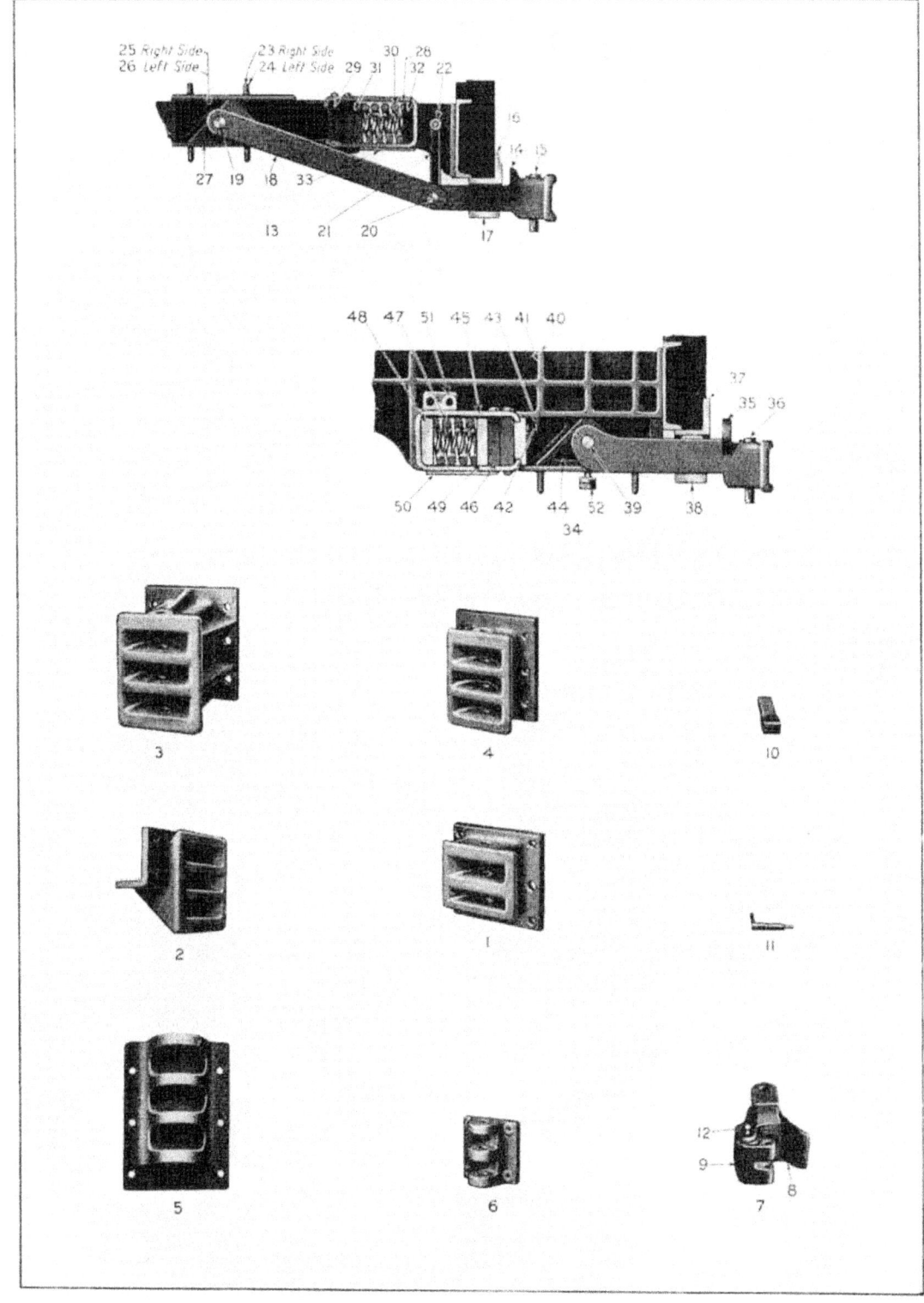

PLATE 15—(Continued)

CODE WORD	FIG.	NAME OF PART	CODE WORD	FIG.	NAME OF PART
Demean	28	Draft gear yoke	*Delude*	41	Draft gear frame, left side
Deduce	29	Draft gear yoke block	*Demerit*	42	Draft gear sliding bar, right side
Deem	30	Draft gear yoke spring	*Demesne*	43	Draft gear sliding bar, left side
Defame	31	Draft gear yoke follower—rear	*Demise*	44	Draft gear friction plate
Defer	32	Draft gear yoke follower—front	*Demur*	45	Draft gear yoke
Defile	33	Draft gear carrier plate	*Denial*	46	Draft gear yoke block
Definable	34	FRICTION DRAFT GEAR COMPLETE	*Denizen*	47	Draft gear yoke spring
			Denote	48	Draft gear yoke follower—rear
Deflect	35	Drawhead			
Deform	36	Drawhead pin	*Dense*	49	Draft gear yoke follower—front
Defray	37	Drawhead guide			
Defy	38	Drawhead carrier	*Dent*	50	Draft gear carrier plate
Deign	39	Draft gear connecting pin	*Denude*	51	Draft gear frame spreader
Dejected	40	Draft gear frame, right side	*Depict*	52	Draft gear tie bar

NOTE.—When ordering repair parts for Friction Draft Gear state whether for front or rear of engine.

We can furnish knuckles for Automatic coupler, either slotted for link or solid with face of following sizes:—9¾ in., 12 in., 14 in., 16 in., 19 in. Specify your requirements.

Automatic couplers are furnished with split shank for coupling in two and three pocket drawheads or square shank for use with friction draft gear. Specify your requirements.

All orders must specify the SHOP NUMBER of locomotive and the "CODE WORD" of part wanted.

In preparing order, read over instructions for ordering carefully to see that you have covered all that is needed to enable us to fill order.

PLATE 16

Crank Shafts, Line Shafts and Accessories, Square Shafts, Sleeve Couplings and Coupling Rings

CODE WORD	FIG.	NAME OF PART	CODE WORD	FIG.	NAME OF PART
Oadal	1	CRANK SHAFT COMPLETE, TWO CYLINDER, TWO TRUCK LOCOMOTIVES	*Oblige*	17	Counterbalance, middle cylinder
			Oblique	18	Counterbalance, front cylinder
Oafish	2	Crank shaft, bare	*Oblivion*	19	Counterbalance yoke
Oaken	3	Crank horn coupling, front	*Oblong*	20	Eccentries, rear cylinder, all style cranks
Oakum	4	Crank horn coupling, rear			
Oasis	5	Counterbalance, rear cylinder	*Obloquy*	21	Eccentries, middle cylinder split, all style cranks, except two cylinder locomotives
Oaten	6	Counterbalance, front cylinder			
Oath	7	Counterbalance yoke			
Obdurate	8	CRANK SHAFT COMPLETE, THREE CYLINDER, TWO TRUCK LOCOMOTIVES	*Obolus*	22	Eccentries, front cylinder, all style cranks
			Oborate	23	ECCENTRIC STRAPS COMPLETE, ONE PAIR, ALL STYLE CRANKS
Obedient	9	Crank shaft, bare			
Obelisk	10	Crank horn coupling, front	*Obscure*	24	Eccentric strap bolts, all style cranks
Obelus	11	Crank horn coupling, rear			
Obese	12	CRANK SHAFT COMPLETE, THREE CYLINDER, THREE AND FOUR TRUCK LOCOMOTIVES	*Obsecrate*	25	LINE SHAFT COMPLETE, FRONT, TWO AND THREE CYLINDER, TWO TRUCK LOCOMOTIVES
Obey	13	Crank shaft, bare	*Observe*	26	Line shaft bare, front
Object	14	Crank horn coupling, front	*Obsidian*	27	Line shaft horn coupling
Objurgate	15	Crank horn coupling, rear	*Obsolete*	28	Line shaft collar, wide
Oblation	16	Counterbalance, rear cylinder	*Obstinate*	29	Line shaft collar, narrow

PLATE 16
Crank Shafts, Line Shafts and Accessories, Square Shafts, Sleeve Couplings and Coupling Rings

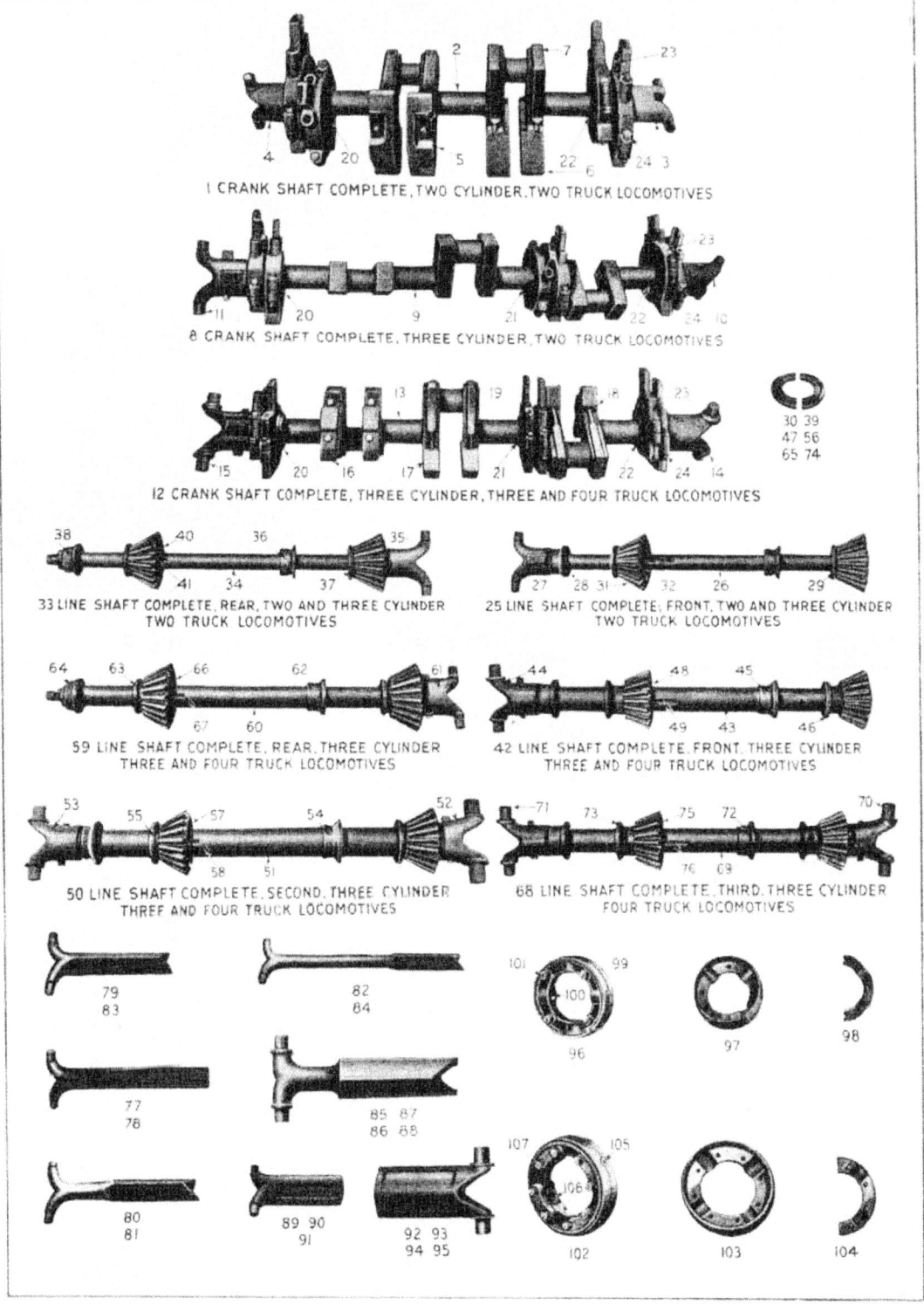

PLATE 16—(Continued)

CODE WORD	FIG.	NAME OF PART	CODE WORD	FIG.	NAME OF PART
Obstruct	30	Line shaft washer	*Olympic*	68	LINE SHAFT COMPLETE, THIRD, THREE CYLINDER, FOUR TRUCK LOCOMOTIVES
Obstrude	31	Line shaft pinion			
Obtuse	32	Line shaft pinion key			
Obverse	33	LINE SHAFT COMPLETE, REAR, TWO AND THREE CYLINDER, TWO TRUCK LOCOMOTIVES	*Ombre*	69	Line shaft, bare, third
			Omega	70	Line shaft horn coupling, front
			Omnibus	71	Line shaft horn coupling, rear
Obvert	34	Line shaft, bare, rear	*Onager*	72	Line shaft collar, wide
Obviate	35	Line shaft horn coupling	*Onion*	73	Line shaft collar, narrow
Obvious	36	Line shaft collar, wide	*Onus*	74	Line shaft washer
Occident	37	Line shaft collar, narrow	*Onyx*	75	Line shaft pinion
Occipital	38	Line shaft collar end	*Opah*	76	Line shaft pinion key
Occiput	39	Line shaft washer	*Opaline*	77	Square shaft, front, Class A locomotives
Occult	40	Line shaft pinion			
Occulty	41	Line shaft pinion key	*Opera*	78	Square shaft, rear, Class A locomotives
Ocean	42	LINE SHAFT COMPLETE, FRONT, THREE CYLINDERS, THREE AND FOUR TRUCK LOCOMOTIVES	*Opiate*	79	Square shaft, rear, Class A locomotives (Used on some locomotives)
Ochre	43	Line shaft, bare	*Oppose*	80	Square shaft, front, Class B locomotives
Octa	44	Line shaft horn coupling			
Octagon	45	Line shaft collar, wide	*Oppress*	81	Square shaft, rear, Class B locomotives
Octant	46	Line shaft collar, narrow			
Octave	47	Line shaft washer	*Opsonic*	82	Square shaft, front, Class C locomotives
Octopod	48	Line shaft pinion			
Octopus	49	Line shaft pinion key	*Optic*	83	Square shaft, second, Class C locomotives
Octoroon	50	LINE SHAFT COMPLETE, SECOND, THREE CYLINDER, THREE AND FOUR TRUCK LOCOMOTIVES	*Optigraph*	84	Square shaft, rear, Class C locomotives
			Opulent	85	Square shaft, front, Class D locomotives
Octuple	51	Line shaft, bare, second	*Oracle*	86	Square shaft, second, Class D locomotives
Ocular	52	Line shaft horn coupling, front			
Oculist	53	Line shaft horn coupling, rear	*Orange*	87	Square shaft, third, Class D locomotives
Oddity	54	Line shaft collar, wide	*Orator*	88	Square shaft, rear, Class D locomotives
Odious	55	Line shaft collar, narrow			
Odium	56	Line shaft washer	*Orbed*	89	Sleeve coupling, front, Class A, B and C locomotives
Offal	57	Line shaft pinion			
Officer	58	Line shaft pinion key	*Orchard*	90	Sleeve coupling, rear, Class A, B and C locomotives
Ogre	59	LINE SHAFT COMPLETE, REAR, THREE CYLINDER, THREE AND FOUR TRUCK LOCOMOTIVES	*Orchid*	91	Sleeve coupling, second, Class C locomotives
			Orcin	92	Sleeve coupling, front, Class D locomotives
Oily	60	Line shaft, bare, rear			
Okra	61	Line shaft horn coupling	*Ordain*	93	Sleeve coupling, second, Class D locomotives
Oleander	62	Line shaft collar, wide			
Oleaster	63	Line shaft collar, narrow	*Ordeal*	94	Sleeve coupling, third, Class D locomotives
Oleate	64	Line shaft collar, end			
Olefiant	65	Line shaft washer	*Organ*	95	Sleeve coupling, rear, Class D locomotives
Oligarch	66	Line shaft pinion			
Olivine	67	Line shaft pinion key			

PLATE 16—(Continued)

CODE WORD	FIG.	NAME OF PART	CODE WORD	FIG.	NAME OF PART
Organist	96	COUPLING RING COMPLETE, FOUR BOLT TYPE (USED ON ALL LOCOMOTIVES WITH CYLINDER SIZE 8 IN. x 12 IN. AND UNDER)	*Ornith*	102	COUPLING RING COMPLETE, EIGHT BOLT TYPE (USED ON ALL LOCOMOTIVES WITH CYLINDER SIZE 10 IN. x 10 IN. AND OVER)
Orgues	97	Outside coupling ring whole for four bolt type	*Orphrey*	103	Outside coupling ring whole, eight bolt type
Orient	98	Inside coupling ring half for four bolt type	*Orpin*	104	Inside coupling ring half, eight bolt type
Origin	99	Coupling ring oil cellar for four bolt type	*Orris*	105	Coupling ring oil cellar, eight bolt type
Oriole	100	Coupling ring bushing for four bolt type	*Orthite*	106	Coupling ring bushing, eight bolt type
Ornate	101	Coupling ring bolts for four bolt type	*Ortho*	107	Coupling ring bolt, eight bolt type

NOTE.—All orders must specify SHOP NUMBER of locomotive and the "CODE WORD" of the part wanted.

In ordering coupling rings complete or coupling ring details, specify truck—whether front, second, third or rear.

For illustration of Class A, B, C and D Shay Locomotives, see Page 4 of this catalogue.

In preparing order, read over instructions for ordering carefully to see that you have covered all that is needed to enable us to fill order.

PLATE 17

Superheater and Details

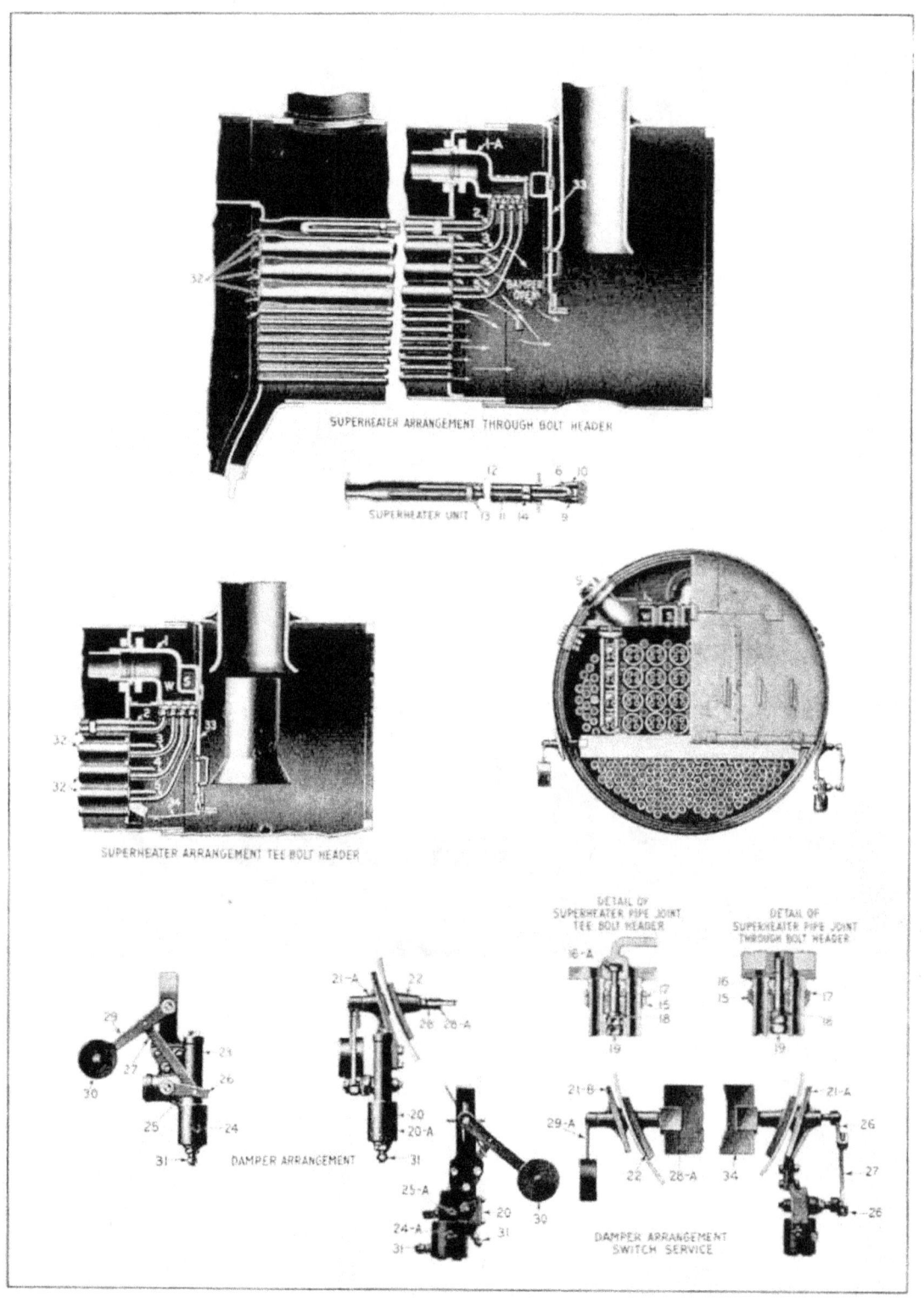

PLATE 17

Superheater and Details

NOTE.—The spare parts for Superheater Equipment illustrated on the opposite page cover parts of standard superheater design for Shay-geared Locomotives. In ordering a spare part it may be found that the part required cannot be identified in all of its details from this list—in such cases, the part most closely approximating the design of the part required should be selected.

In all cases, the following information should be given on orders for Superheater spare parts: Owner's Name and Address. Builder's No. of Engine. List No. or Drawing of Part. No. of Parts required. All parts should be ordered direct from THE SUPERHEATER CO., 17 East 42nd St., New York City, N. Y.

CODE WORD	FIG.	NAME OF PART	NO. PER ENGINE
Udder	1-A	Modified through Bolt Header	1
Ugly	1	Tee Bolt Header	1
Uhlan	2	Unit Shape No. 1	1—for each Unit in top row
Ukase	3	Unit Shape No. 2	1—for each Unit in 2nd row
Ulcer	4	Unit Shape No. 3	1—for each Unit in 3rd row
Ulna	5	Unit Shape No. 4	1—for each Unit in 4th row
Ulster	6	Cast Steel Return Bend, Style N for Bituminous Coal	1—for each Unit with Cast Steel Return Bends
Ultima	9	Unit Pipe No. 1	1—for each Unit
Ultra	10	Unit Pipe No. 2	1—for each Unit
Umbel	11	Unit Pipe No. 3	1—for each Unit
Umber	12	Unit Pipe No. 4	1—for each Unit
Umbo	13	Unit Pipe Support	For units 13' long or less, 1 for each unit — For units 13' long, 2 for each unit
Umlaut	14	Pipe Band	1—for each Unit
Unbend	15	Unit Clamp	1—for each Unit
Unchain	16	Unit Bolt for through Bolt Header	1—for each Unit
Uncivil	16-A	Unit Bolt for Tee bolt Header	1—for each Unit
Uncle	17	Unit Pipe End Washer	2—for each Unit
Unction	18	Unit Clamp Bolt Washer	1—for each Unit
Undercut	19	Unit Bolt Nuts—Hex. Faced	2—for each Unit
Undo	20	Damper Cylinder Complete—Vertical Type	1
Undue	20-A	Damper Cylinder Complete—Horizontal Type	1
Undulate	21	Damper Shaft Bearing, and Cylinder Support for Horizontal Damper Cylinder (Not illustrated)	1
Unduly	21-A	Damper Shaft Bearing, and Cylinder Support for Vertical Damper Cylinder	1
	21-B	Damper Shaft Bearing—Outside	
Unearth	22	Damper Shaft Bearing—Inside	2
Uneasy	23	Damper Cylinder Body	1
Unequal	24	Damper Cylinder Piston (Pipe connection at bottom)	1
Uneven	24-A	Damper Cylinder Piston (Pipe connection at side)	1
Unfair	25	Damper Cylinder Arm—Inside (Pipe connection at bottom)	1
Unfelt	25-A	Damper Cylinder Arm—Inside (Pipe connection at side)	1
Unfetter	26	Damper Cylinder Arm—Outside	1
Unfix	27	Damper Link	1
Unfold	28	Damper Shaft—(Jaw 2" wide)	1
Unfurl	28-A	Damper Shaft—(Jaw 4" wide)	2
Ungear	29	Damper Shaft Counterweight Arm with Jaw	1
Ungard	29-A	Damper Shaft Counterweight Arm without Jaw	1
Ungirt	30	Damper Counterweight	1
Ungulate	31	Damper Pipe Union	2
Unicorn	32	Superheater Flue	1—for each Unit
Unify	33	Deflecting Plate	1

PLATE 18

Feed Water Heater

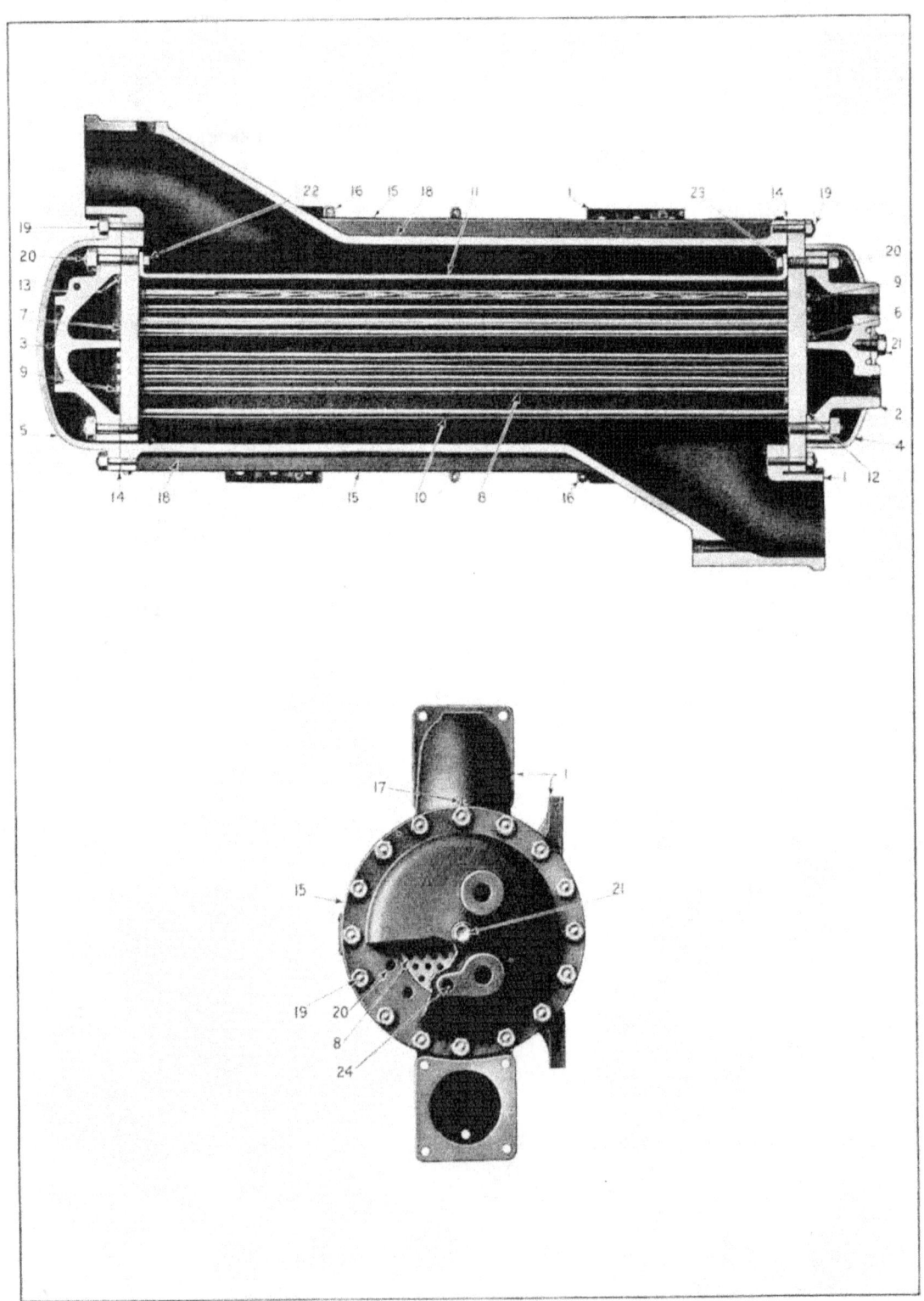

PLATE 17—(Continued)

CODE WORD	FIG.	NAME OF PART	NO. PER ENGINE
Uniped	34	Damper	1
Unjust	35	Damper Pipe Fitting (Not illustrated)	2

The following Tools and Equipment are not illustrated. Tools are used for maintenance purposes:

CODE WORD	FIG.	NAME OF PART	
Unravel	36	Soft Metal Grinding Mould—for maintaining contour of Unit Joints	
Unrivalled	37	Prosser—for proper setting of flues in Tube Sheet	
Unroll	38	Rolls—for rolling of flues in Tube Sheet	
Unseal	39	Emergency Clamp and Washer, permitting replacement of these parts without removing units	
Unyoke	40	Electric Pyrometer—A fixture as important as the steam gauge, which indicates steam temperatures	
Upper	41	Unit Pipe Emergency Washer—Used only in connection with emergency clamp	

PLATE 18

Feed Water Heater

CODE WORD	FIG.	NAME OF PART	CODE WORD	FIG.	NAME OF PART
Hale	1	Body	*Harden*	13	Gasket (Floating Header)
Hallow	2	Main Header	*Haricot*	14	Gasket (Body)
Halter	3	Floating Header	*Harmel*	15	Jacket
Halve	4	Main Header Casing	*Harness*	16	Jacket Clamp
Hamlet	5	Floating Header Casing	*Harp*	17	Jacket Bolts
Hamper	6	Main Tube Plate	*Harrier*	18	Lagging
Hanger	7	Floating Tube Plate	*Harsh*	19	Body Studs
Hank	8	Tubes	*Harvest*	20	Header Studs
Hapless	9	Agitators	*Hasp*	21	Casing Bolt
Haptic	10	Tube Nest Guards	*Hatch*	22	Baffle Bolts
Harass	11	Baffle	*Heckle*	23	Baffle Bolts
Harbor	12	Gasket (Main Header)	*Hesitate*	24	Drain Valve

The following tools and equipment are not illustrated. Tools are used for maintenance purposes only.

CODE WORD	NO.	NAME OF PART	CODE WORD	NO.	NAME OF PART
Habit	1	Prosser	*Hail*	8	Expanding Plugs
Hack	1	Backing out Rod	*Haggle*	1	Test Ring (with Clamps)
Haddock	1	Special Reamer	*Haggard*	1	Bevelling Plug

TABLE OF CONTENTS

Plate No.	Description
1	Cylinder and Cylinder Details
2	Cylinder and Cylinder Details
3	Valve Motion and Details
4	Steam and Bottom Brackets
5	Steam and Bottom Brackets
6	Boiler, Boiler Details and Outside Fittings
7	Inside Cab Fittings, Smoke Box Arrangement, Ash Pan Details
8	Inside Cab Fittings, Smoke Box Arrangement, Ash Pan Details
9	Stacks, Grates and Details
10	Trucks and Truck Details
11	Trucks and Truck Details
12	Tank Valve, Syphon and Details
13	Engine Frames and Frame Details
14	Engine Frames and Frame Details
15	Draft Gear, Drawheads and Automatic Couplers
16	Crank Shafts, Line Shafts and Accessories, Square Shafts, Sleeve Couplings and Coupling Rings
17	Superheater and Details
18	Feed Water Heater

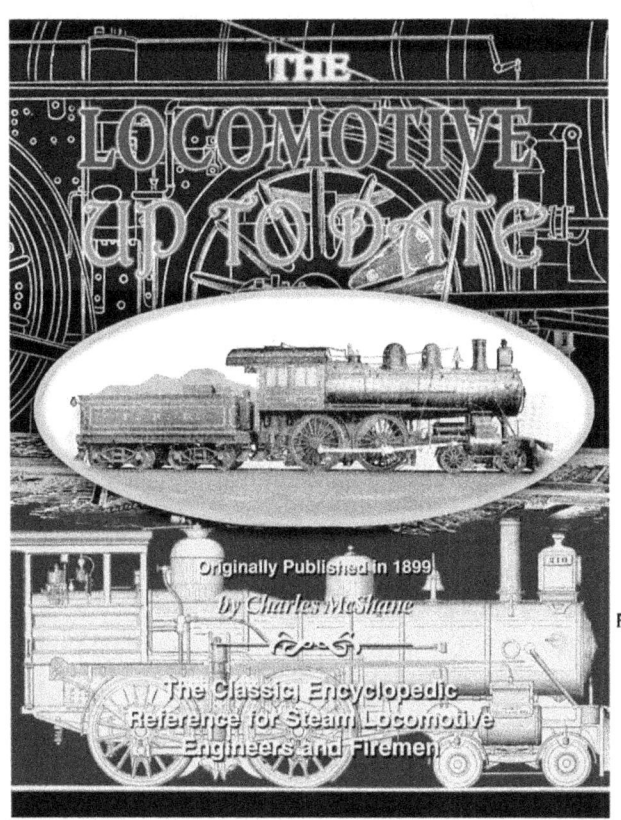

When it was originally published in 1899, **The Locomotive Up to Date** was hailed as "...the most definitive work ever published concerning the mechanism that has transformed the American nation: the steam locomotive." Filled with over 700 pages of text, diagrams and photos, this remains one of the most important railroading books ever written. From steam valves to sanders, trucks to side rods, it's a treasure trove of information, explaining in easy-to-understand language how the most sophisticated machines of the 19th Century were operated and maintained. This new edition is an exact duplicate of the original. Reformatted as an easy-to-read 8.5x11 volume, it's delightful for railroad enthusiasts of all ages.

Originally printed in 1898 and then periodically revised, **The Motorman...and His Duties** served as the definitive training text for a generation of streetcar operators. A must-have for the trolley or train enthusiast, it is also an important source of information for museum staff and docents. Lavishly illustrated with numerous photos and black and white line drawings, this affordable reprint contains all of the original text. Includes chapters on trolley car types and equipment, troubleshooting, brakes, controllers, electricity and principles, electric traction, multi-car control and has a convenient glossary in the back. If you've ever operated a trolley car, or just had an electric train set, this is a terrific book for your shelf!

ALSO NOW AVAILABLE FROM PERISCOPEFILM.COM!

©2008-2010 Periscope Film LLC
All Rights Reserved
ISBN #978-1-935327-92-9   1-935327-92-5
www.PeriscopeFilm.com

www.ingramcontent.com/pod-product-compliance
Lightning Source LLC
Chambersburg PA
CBHW080456170426
43196CB00016B/2824